Queridos Mama + Papa:
¡ Todavía no hay
nietos ... pero por
si acaso ! Que lo disfruten
los quiere !
12/98

Letter to
My Grandchild

Letter to
My Grandchild

Edited by Liv Ullmann

 Atlantic Monthly Press / New York

Photo Credits: *Fernando Arrabal* Jean-Pierre Couderc, 1981 (Polfoto); *Vladimir Ashkenazy* Kimmo Mäntylä (Nordfoto); *Harry Belafonte* (Nordfoto); *Gro Harlem Brundtland* 1995 (Nordfoto); *Barbara Bush* courtesy of Barbara Bush; *Jimmy Carter* courtesy of Jimmy Carter; *Jung Chang* by Peter R. Simpkin; *Leo Cherne* courtesy of Leo Cherne; *Leonard Cohen* Liselotte Sabroe, 1992 (Nordfoto); *Walter Cronkite* Svend Aage Martensen, 1993 (Nordfoto); *The Dalai Lama* Duane Burleson, 1994 (Nordfoto); *Umberto Eco* 1983 (Polfoto); *Oriana Fallaci* 1981 (Polfoto); *Marilyn French* Jan Erik Henriksson, 1994 (Nordfoto); *Jostein Gaarder* Sine Fiig, 1996 (Nordfoto); *Nadine Gordimer* Morten Juhl, 1997 (Nordfoto); *Katharine Graham* courtesy of Corbis-Bettmann; *Václav Havel* Esa Pyysalo, 1995 (Nordfoto); *Thor Heyerdahl* Lise Åserud, 1994 (Nordfoto); *Doris Lessing* 1988 (Nordfoto); *Astrid Lindgren* Jacob Forsell, 1987 (Polfoto); *Nelson Mandela* 1995 (Nordfoto); *Martina Navratilova* 1993 (Polfoto); *Shimon Peres* Brian Hendler, 1996 (Nordfoto); *Aleksandar Soknic* courtesy of The International Resuce Committee in Belgrade and Aleksandar Soknic; *Karlheinz Stockhausen* Leif Weckström, 1990 (Nordfoto); *Desmond Tutu* Rashid Lombard, 1994 (Nordfoto); *Liv Ullmann* Leif R. Jansson, 1996 (Nordfoto); *Jørn Utzon* 1994 (Nordfoto); *Lech Wałęsa* Bax Lindhardt, 1996 (Nordfoto); *Andrew Weil* by John R. Ziemann; *Fay Weldon* 1988 (Polfoto); *Elie Wiesel* Claus Bjorn, 1991 (Polfoto); *Simon Wiesenthal* Ronald Zak, 1996 (Nordfoto)

Translation credits: *Jostein Gaarder* translated from the Norwegian by Barbara J. Haveland; *Lech Wałęsa* translated from the Polish by Bill Johnston; *Simon Wiesenthal* translated from the German by Layla Aker and Adam Becker; *Elie Wiesel* translated from the French by Layla Aker and Adam Becker

Published by appointment with Aschehoug Dansk Forlag A/S
Published simultaneously in Canada
Printed in the United States of America

Acknowledgments:

The following texts were donated to the book:

Fernando Arrabal, drawing (partly in color)

Gro Harlem Brundlandt, excerpt from the *Closing Address, Fourth World Conference for Women*, Beijing, September 15, 1995

Umberto Eco, *Letter to my Son*, 1964

Oriana Fallaci, excerpt from the book, *Letter to a Child Never Born*
Copyright © 1975 RCS Rizzoli Libri S.p.A., Milano
Copyright © 1994 RCS Libri & Grandi Opere S.p.A., Milano

Vaclav Havel, speech from *United Nations World Summit for Children*, New York, September 30, 1990 and *The Anatomy of Hate*, Oslo 1990

Astrid Lindgren, "Susy Spry", reprinted by permission of the author

Nelson Mandela, speech from *The Eminent Persons Group Meeting in the Study on the Impact of Armed Conflict on Children*, January 29, 1996

Liv Ullmann's letter, originally published in *The International Herald Tribune*, 1993

FIRST EDITION

Design by Laura Hammond Hough

Library of Congress Cataloging-in-Publication Data

Letter to my grandchild / edited by Liv Ullmann.
    p.   cm.
    ISBN 0-87113-728-3
    1. Grandparents—Correspondence. 2. Celebrities—Correspondence.
    3. Conduct of life. 4. Quality of life. 5. Social action.
    I. Ullmann, Liv.
    HQ759.9.L478   1998
    306.874'5—dc21   98-26864
                                     CIP

Atlantic Monthly Press
841 Broadway
New York, NY 10003

98 99 00 01 10 9 8 7 6 5 4 3 2 1

Contents

Letter to
My Grandchild

The Letter I Sent All Around the World

I am writing to you to ask you to contribute to a book project entitled *Letter to My Grandchild* which I am working on at the moment.

The book will be published for the benefit of the Women's Commission for Refugee Women and Children, a division of the International Rescue Committee. The Women's Commission is dedicated to speaking out on behalf of the millions of women and children around the world who have been uprooted by civil strife, war, persecution and famine. Its goal is to improve the lives of refugee women and children through a vigorous and comprehensive program of public education and advocacy.

The idea behind the book is that a number of prominent personalities in the world, people who are known for their engagement for a better world, will write a personal letter to their own grandchild—or to *all* grandchildren.

The letter may be about something very specific, something you would like to tell about your own experience. It could be about important events in your life, or values that you care about—or it may be a letter about the possibilities or challenges or threats which your grandchild's life may contain or a letter about the kind of world you would like your grandchild to live in. As specific and personal as possible—and of course with love.

On my grandmother's lap I told her: "I love you." She said: "Do you know what hurts me?" The little girl—me—answered: "No." And then the older woman said: "How can you love me—if you don't know what hurts me?"

May I with this book thank my grandmother, Dagmar Ullmann, for what she gave me.

Liv Ullmann

Letter to
My Grandchild

Letter to
My Grandchild

Fernando Arrabal

PLAYWRIGHT AND NOVELIST Fernando Arrabal was born in 1932 in Spain. He studied law in Madrid and drama in Paris, then settled permanently in France. His first play, *Pique-nique en campagne* (*Picnic on the Battlefield*), established him in the tradition of the Theater of the Absurd. His books include *The Red Virgin* and *The Tower Struck by Lightning*. His plays include *And they put handcuffs on the flowers* and *Guernica*. Arrabal has also written and directed several films.

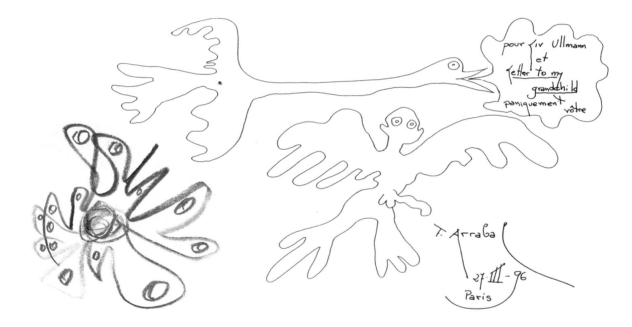

Fernando Arrabal

Vladimir
Ashkenazy

PIANIST AND CONDUCTOR Vladimir
Ashkenazy was born in Russia in 1937 and graduated from the Moscow Conservatory
in 1960. He left the Soviet Union in 1963 and has since made numerous recordings and
performed all over the world. He became musical director of the Royal Philharmonic
Orchestra in 1987. Since 1989, Ashkenazy has been chief conductor of Deutches
Symphonie-Orchester Berlin.

I wish that my grandson will learn early to distinguish between good and evil.
I wish him to be tolerant but not of evil.
I wish that he will be honest to himself and to others.
I wish that he will never do unto others what he would not have done to himself.
I wish him to be a realist with vision. Rather than thinking of success, let him always try to do his best, whatever he is doing.
I wish him to remember that freedom is not a license but a duty and to be considerate to others.

—*Vladimir Ashkenazy*

Harry Belafonte

SINGER AND ACTOR Harry Belafonte was born in Harlem in 1927 but spent his childhood in Jamaica. After joining the U. S. Navy for two years, he settled in New York, where he became involved in the American Negro Theater and the Dramatic Workshop. In 1955, he became a Broadway star in *Three for Tonight,* and his recording of "Calypso" was the first pop album to sell 1 million copies. His albums "Banana Boat Song" and "Jamaica Farewell" were also popular sensations. He later starred in the films *Buck and the Preacher* and *Uptown Saturday Night.* Belafonte is also known for championing the civil rights of black Americans, and in 1982 he received the Martin Luther King Peace Prize.

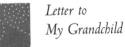

Letter to My Grandchild

Dear Rachel,

Although I love you very much and have always welcomed the opportunity to be in your company, no experience we have shared has been quite as joyous as our little sojourn throughout parts of Europe. How wonderful it was to visit all the places we have been and to have seen the many things we saw, especially through your eyes. It will stay with me forever. All the years I had visited Paris and had attended functions at the Louvre, I had never seen the *Mona Lisa,* and to finally have done so during the afternoon we spent there was a wonderful experience.

As we moved about from place to place I was once again struck by the uniqueness of each country and city and as much alike as human beings are in so many ways, it is a wondrous thing to be touched by the power and the beauty of our differences. So often things that are different are things that are feared. How sad that we are unable to see that in difference there is opportunity, that in difference we find the opportunity to learn and to be creative and most of all that in the acceptance of difference we nourish our own humanity.

The world that you will inherit will be deeply troubled and divided. There is a great sadness in that fact, especially for those of us who have struggled so hard to rechart the course of human encounter by our efforts and attempts to make this world a more joyous place.

My friend and mentor, Paul Robeson, once said, "Regardless of what we contribute, in the final analysis every generation must be responsible for itself. The future of our planet, of our world and how it goes will knock loudly on your door, and on the doors of others of your generation for solutions to its problems. When you answer the door do not be frightened by the difference you may see standing there. Examine it and understand what it is, for it may be bringing you a gift."

I look forward to the time when we can make yet another journey.
Love,

"Grand pere"
Harry

**Gro
Harlem
Brundtland**

NORWEGIAN STATESWOMAN AND
first woman prime minister of Norway, Gro Harlem Brundtland was born in Oslo in
1931. She studied medicine at Oslo and Harvard, and in 1974 she was elected minister
for the environment. In 1981 she was elected Labor Party leader and prime minister, a
post she regained in 1986 and again in 1990. In 1987 she chaired the World
Commission on Environment and Development, which produced the report *Our
Common Future*. In 1988 she was awarded the Third World Foundation Prize for
leadership in environmental issues.

*Letter to
My Grandchild*

Every second a baby boy and baby girl are born into this world of diversity and inequality. They all deserve love and care, a future and opportunities. There is nothing so thoroughly, so unconditionally trusting as the look in the eyes of a newborn girl or boy child. From that privilege, we must depart, and make ourselves worthy of the look in those eyes.

✻   ✻   ✻   ✻

We came here to answer the call of billions of women who have lived, and of billions of women who will live. Women will no longer accept the role of second-rate citizens.

All history of liberation struggles tells us that life, freedom, equality and opportunity have never been given. They have always been taken. Women cannot maintain the illusion that someone else is going to do the job and establish our equality with men. Women, and men working with us, men who understand, we all must fight for that freedom.

Today we know that women's contribution to the economy are decisive for growth and social development. We know that countries will continue to live in poverty if women remain under the heel of oppression. We know the costs of a continuing genderized apartheid.

Today, there isn't a single country in the world—not one—where men and women enjoy equal opportunities. So we must go back from Beijing
go back to the shantytowns of Third World megacities,
go back to the croplands at the desert's edge in Africa,
to the indigenous communities of Latin-American rain forests
go home to change values and attitudes.
But not only there.
no, we must go to the boardrooms,
to the suburbia of Europe and North America.

to all of our local communities.

to our governments

and to the United Nations' headquarters.

We agree that women's education is essential. This year's Human Development Report makes it emphatically clear: The economic returns on investing in women's education are fully comparable to those for men. But the social returns from educating women far exceed those of educating men.

Schooling of girls is one of the unlocking keys to development.

* * * *

I have heard the following allegation from a country not to be named: "The West, to be frank, is attempting to impose its cultural pattern as an international model."

Wrong—most countries are today strongly defending their own cultures. And there is more respect and mutual understanding of the value of other cultures and religions than ever before.

But the point is a different one: There are limits to the practices that countries can expect the international community to accept, or condone, even when such practices have deep cultural roots. This is where human rights enter the picture.

Violence against women, also domestic violence, can be said to be part of a "cultural pattern," in most countries including my own.

And clearly, freedom from violence and coercion must apply also in the sexual sphere of life. This conference has rightly made clear what the existing human rights must mean in practice.

The state becomes an accomplice if violence against women is seen as a separate cultural category of behavior extraneous to the realm of justice and law enforcement.

There are often ancient root causes of such practices. But they are committed by people who live today. Why are there astonishingly more boys than girls in certain countries? The question may be unpleasant for governments, who do not encourage these crimes. But we will all be found guilty if we close our eyes.

Letter to
My Grandchild

Why are girl children given less and poorer food than their brothers? Why do they receive less health care and less education? Why are they subjected to the horrible tradition of sexual exploitation?

Ingrained, centuries-old attitudes are not easily changed, but these which I have mentioned must be. The task requires vigorous action on the part of governments, religious groups and private, nongovernmental organizations.

Greater equality in the family is to the good for men, women and children. The allegation that this conference is against motherhood and family is plainly absurd.

Today, we recognize that povety has a gender bias. Increasingly, poverty discriminates between men and women.

The myth that men are the economic providers and women, mainly, are mothers and caregivers in the family has now been thoroughly refuted. This family pattern has never been the norm, except in a narrow middle-class segment.

Women have always worked, in all societies—and at all times. As a rule they have worked harder than men, and, as a rule, without pay and acknowledgment. Their contribution has been essential for national economies as well as to their families.

But overlooking women's contribution to the economy has had more severe damaging effects. Often women cannot even obtain a modest loan to become more independent and productive. In many countries, women own nothing, they inherit nothing and are unable to offer security. On top of that laws often work against them.

No, women will not become more empowered merely because we want them to be, but through change of legislation, increased information and by redirecting resources.

Ministers of finance and planning may rue their former practice faced with what Beijing says about the economic role of women. Unleashing women from the chains of poverty is not only a question of justice. It is a question of sound economic growth and improved welfare for everyone.

Gro Harlem Brundtland

Barbara
Bush

HUMANITARIAN AND FORMER First Lady Barbara Pierce Bush grew up in Rye, New York, where she met and later married George Bush. Throughout her years in public life Mrs. Bush has volunteered in and supported hundreds of charity and humanitarian causes. However, her primary cause is literacy and in 1990 she helped develop the Barbara Bush Foundation for Family Literacy. She is the author of *C. Fred's Story, Millie's Book,* and *Barbara Bush: A Memoir,* her best-selling autobiography.

Letter to
My Grandchild

Dear George P., Noelle, Jenna, Barbara, Sam, Jebby, Lauren, Pierce, Marshall, Ellie, Ashley, Walker, Robert and GiGi,

I can think of no better lesson to teach you than to try—and oh boy, how hard it is—to always find the good in people and not the bad. Remember that nobody is perfect. Certainly not me. So LOOK FOR THE GOOD IN OTHERS. Forget the other.

Clara Barton, founder and president of the Red Cross, was once reminded of a wrong a friend had done to her years earlier. "Don't you remember?" the friend asked. "No," replied Clara firmly. "I distinctly remember forgetting that." Not bad advice. Take a lesson from your Gampy. He says when I remind him that someone has been hateful, "Isn't it better to make a friend rather than an enemy?" He's right, too.

There are a few other important lessons I want to share with you as well.

Don't talk about money . . . either having it or not having it. It is embarrassing for others and quite frankly vulgar. DO NOT BUY SOMETHING THAT YOU CANNOT AFFORD. YOU DO NOT NEED IT. If you really need something and can't afford it . . . for heaven's sake call home. That's what family are all about.

Do not try to live up to your neighbors. They won't look down on you if you don't have two television sets. They will look down on you if you buy things that you cannot afford, and they will know it! They are only interested in their possessions, not yours.

Be sure that you pay people back. If you have dinner at their house or they take you out, have them back, but remember you don't need the expensive thing. You can make the best spaghetti in the world. People love to come to your home. Plan ahead and it will be fun.

Value your friends. They are your most valuable asset.

Remember loyalty is a two-way street. It goes up and down. So be loyal to those people who are loyal to you. Your Gampy is the best example of two-way loyalty that I know.

For heaven's sake enjoy life. Don't cry over things that were or things that aren't. Enjoy what you have now to the fullest. In all honesty you really only have two choices:

Letter to
My Grandchild

you can like what you do *OR* you can dislike it. I choose to like it, and what fun I have had. The other choice is no fun and people do not want to be around a whiner. We can always find people who are worse off, and we don't have to look far! Help them and forget yourself!

I would certainly say, above all, seek God. He will come to you if you look. There is absolutely *NO* downside. Please expose your children and set a good example for them by going to church. We, your Gampy and I, have tried to live as Christian a life as we can. We certainly have not been perfect. Maybe you can be! Keep trying.

All my love,
Ganny—
(Barbara Bush)

Jimmy Carter

FORMER PRESIDENT JIMMY Carter is chairman of the nonprofit Carter Center in Atlanta, which advances peace and health in nations and neighborhoods throughout the world.

A letter to my grandchildren: Jason, James, John, Sarah, Rosemary, Sarah Elizabeth, Joshua, Margaret, Jeremy, and Jamie.

You were lucky enough to be born in a great and powerful nation, and in a family that has had all the advantages of a modern society. All of you will have different ambitions in life, largely depending on what career you choose for yourselves. You will wish to be successful, whether as a doctor, lawyer, teacher, carpenter, athlete, computer programmer, painter, actor—or just a peanut farmer. There will certainly be times when you will feel that you have failed to realize your fondest dreams.

It is important to remember that success in life is not measured by our bank account, the size of our house or automobile, the number of times our names are in the news, or how long we live. Measured on an ultimate scale, the measurements of success are quite different from those we might normally consider.

When the members of the early church in Corinth asked Saint Paul to name for them the important things, those that never change, he gave them a strange answer: "What is unseen is eternal."

We can see bank statements, newspaper headlines, material possessions, and bountiful harvests. What are the invisible things that outweigh all our momentary strivings and troubles? You can make your own list, perhaps, but Paul was speaking of lives committed to or filled with justice, peace, humility, service, forgiveness, compassion, and love.

There is something remarkable about this list of life's top priorities. As we deal with the people around us, whether just a few or thousands, we can see that every one of us has all the talent, intelligence, eloquence, and influence that we need.

Jimmy Carter

Jung Chang

WRITER JUNG CHANG was born in 1952 in Sichuan, China. During the Cultural Revolution, her family was persecuted by the authorities and she herself was exiled to the edge of the Himalayas. In 1991 she published *Wild Swans,* a book describing the tragic circumstances surrounding her family under Communist rule. Jung Chang left China in 1978 and now lives in London.

Letter to My Grandchild

Dear Granddaughter,

I am leaving you this letter with a book that I have written, a book that means a great deal to me, and a book I long for you to read. It is the true story of women in our family—my own grandmother, my mother, and myself, about our lives in twentieth-century China. In the book, *Wild Swans*, your great-grandmother—my mother—is a central character, and I hope that when you come to read it, she is still alive and well, and that you have had a chance to know her. I wanted now to tell you something more about her, about how I started writing *Wild Swans* because of her, and about how I came to understand her as a result of writing the book. I will be so happy if, after reading *Wild Swans*, and this letter, you appreciate her and love her as I do.

My mother lives in Chengdu, the capital of Sichuan, in the heartland of China. I grew up there, and in 1978, at the age of 26, left for Britain. Mao Zedong had died, China was beginning to open up, and I became one of the first people to be allowed out. Ten years later, my mother came to London to stay with me. It was her first trip abroad. I wanted her to enjoy herself thoroughly, and spent much of my spare time taking her out. After a while, I noticed she was not having the time of her life. Something was on her mind; she was restless. I was puzzled, as this was quite out of character.

Born in 1931, my mother was the daughter of a warlord general and his concubine. She became a Communist underground fighter when she was 15: she led student movements, and smuggled military information out of her city during the civil war between the Communists and the Kuomintang. Once she was arrested and put up against a wall and the man next to her was shot dead. When the Communists took power, when she was barely in her 20s, she was put in charge of education, health, and entertainment for half a million people in Chengdu. In the Cultural Revolution (1966–76), she refused to denounce my father, who was one of the few senior officials who stood up to Mao. She was detained, made to kneel on broken glass, tortured, and exiled to a labour camp. In that decade of upheaval, it was my mother who protected her five young children—and my father. Against extraordinary odds, she escaped to Peking, saw Premier Zhou En Lai, and ensured my father's release from prison. Through her ordeals, my mother never lost her composure.

But one spring Saturday in my flat in Notting Hill Gate in London, she let her unshed tears fall. That morning, she declined a shopping trip to Harrods and settled at my black dining table, on which a bouquet of golden daffodils shone. Cupping a mug of jasmine tea with both hands, she began to talk about my father.

She was a newlywed eighteen-year-old and was on a march of over 1,000 miles from Manchuria to Sichuan with an army unit. The rules said that having just joined the revolution, she had to walk, while my father, who was a senior officer, was entitled to ride. He would not give her a lift because this was against regulations and would have been seen as nepotism, which the Communists had vowed to eliminate. The outcome was that my mother suffered a miscarriage and lost her first child. I was struck by the bitterness in her voice: I had always assumed she was happily married because I had seen her fighting so hard for my father in the Cultural Revolution and suffering atrociously without a murmur.

I pressed her to tell me more, and saw that my interest and sympathy smoothed out the little lines of uncertainty on her face. She had obviously not been too sure how I would react: she knew how much I loved my father, and by Chinese standards, his behaviour was to be admired, not to be complained about.

My mother talked every day for months. Her earlier restlessness was gone completely. There were many shocks—and revelations. Things I had not understood before suddenly fell into place. I had had some vague memory of being in a state nursery and my mother sitting by my bedside late one night. I had not seen her for a very long time. I gripped her hand and refused to go to sleep because I was worried she might disappear again. Then she pulled herself away and left, not turning her head to my screams. I was so angry with her that I was ill for days.

It was in this period that I developed a series of strange high fevers, stomach pains, and heart troubles that plagued my childhood, some still shadowing my adult life. Now I learned the painful truth that my mother could not explain: she had been detained under suspicion of being a "counterrevolutionary" when I was three.

Letter to
My Grandchild

Tourism became the backdrop of our conversations. As we travelled to the Isle of Skye and Lake Lugano, she would talk in the car, during walks, and halfway through the night. When I was working, she would stay at home and speak into a tape recorder. Here, outside all the social and political confines of China, she was able to open her mind and her heart. Her stories were perfectly organised. She remembered things accurately because over the decades she had had to go through them again and again, in great detail, for her interrogators. At one point, 15 people were sent all over China to investigate her. By the time she left London, she had done 60 hours of tape recordings. It was to preserve these memories that I started writing the stories of our lives and that of my grandmother through the turbulence of 20th century China.

For two and a half years, *Wild Swans* dominated both our lives. When the book was nearly completed, one bright spring morning in 1991, an exceptionally short letter came from my mother: the book may not sell and people may not pay much attention to it, but I was not to be disheartened; I had made her a happy woman because writing the book had brought us closer. This alone, she said, was enough for her. It was typical of my mother to anticipate disaster and to try to protect me. But this time, I was unusually moved because I had lived with the emotional turmoil and historical trials that had tempered her character. I had come to a new degree of respect and love for my mother.

Wild Swans turned out to be a success. When I telephoned my mother in Chengdu about the foreign-language editions (there are 25 of them so far), the best-seller lists, and the awards, she showed no surprise. Only pride filled her voice. I could sense her appreciation and contentment without her saying anything: she had found understanding not only in her daughter, but also in millions of readers all over the world.

My dear granddaughter, I hope you enjoy *Wild Swans.*

Your grandmother,
Jung Chang

Leo Cherne

HUMANITARIAN LEO CHERNE has served as economic adviser to almost every U.S. president since 1948, and since 1951 he has been chairman of the International Rescue Committee, an organization which functions on four continents to assist refugees of totalitarian governments. In 1973 he was appointed to the president's Foreign Intelligence Advisory Board. Cherne was awarded the United States Medal of Freedom in 1983, the highest award a president can offer a civilian. In 1989 he received the Jefferson Award, as the U. S. citizen who contributed most to his country.

Letter to
My Grandchild

Dear Erica:

What a wonderful time to be born. You have already missed several events which had their share of sorrow and pain.

Were the last two generations yours, you might have seen, and in fact, in some way been involved in two wars. Perhaps the most dreadful act of human savagery clouded the entire century which you are about to escape. It seems likely that no such horror will again befall the human race.

But the days ahead for you will not be quiet ones, and in some ways I am not unhappy about that. Tranquillity is not my wish for you, because you will not grow to the potential which lies ahead of you if the coming days were truly tranquil. Indeed, a remarkable period is coming.

There is a word you will increasingly hear . . . the millennium. The first signs of this occurrence have already begun to throw their shadow, even though there are still three more years to go before the calendar heralds the arrival of the year 2000. The world has already witnessed several miraculous events.

We have seen a passionate outpouring of grief and adoration on the tragic death of a princess. Less remarkable, and more deserving, was the utterly unprecedented outpouring of international expression of gratitude. We expressed sentiments which defy language. We expressed a collective guilt to one who sought to heal the poorest of the poor.

Dear little one, in less than three years 2,000 years of human history will be behind us. A new millennium will be yours to experience.

This remarkable threshold will be the second millennium of our history in which reasonably accurate records have recorded human behavior.

The passage of 1,000 years has been a curious time. For reasons of which we cannot be certain, behavior as that threshold is crossed is remarkable. It defies logic. The human soul behaves with great and unheralded passion. Quite unpredictable events find us responding in a way that is unexpectedly passionate.

In retrospect, we learn that a need to give, to experience sacrifice, has come upon us. A semblance of saintliness is found. To me, the needs of the poorest of the poor is an obligation we somehow aspire to.

The best in human experience is adored. Love, faith, decency are venerated. We must somehow purge our guilts.

We are crossing a mysterious time. Our future is unknown. The guilts of the past must be purged if the promise of tomorrow may be earned.

This, dear Erica, is ahead of us. It is the millennium.

Fifty-three years ago, as I tried to look into your mother's future, I dedicated a book to her. I dedicated my speculations with the words I now wish to close this letter to you with:

With the deep hope that the rest of your life will be linked to the possibilities, not chained to the probabilities.

With my love,

Poppy

Leonard Cohen

SINGER-SONGWRITER, POET, and author Leonard Cohen was born in 1934 in Montreal. He wrote his first book of poetry, *Let Us Compare Mythologies*, in 1956 soon after graduating from McGill University. A highly popular poet and songwriter, he is also the author of several novels, including *Beautiful Losers*.

To the child of my child,

I may not be around when you read this but I want you to know that this morning I walked on a path and I could see the full moon above the pine trees. It was very bright and round and full and it made me very happy to see it. Someday you will be watching that same moon. I hope it makes you happy too.

Love,

Your Grandfather

Walter Cronkite

AMERICAN TV CORRESPONDENT

Walter Cronkite was born in 1916. He graduated from the University of Texas, then worked as a correspondent for United Press for eleven years. After reporting the German surrender, Cronkite remained in Europe, where he was chief UP correspondent at the Nuremberg trials. He returned to the United States to work as a correspondent and anchorman for CBS in 1950.

In addition to his ongoing assignments as a special correspondent for CBS, Cronkite hosts many public affairs and cultural programs for PBS and syndication. He has received numerous awards and honors, including the Presidential Medal of Freedom in 1981.

To my grandchildren:

As I write this, we are just some two years away from the beginning of the twenty-first century since the birth of Christ. Much is being made of the magical date since the farewell to an old century and the welcome to a new after all does come only once every hundred years. Our literature these days is filled with predictions of the great scientific and technological inventions to come, with fantasies of what the world will be like a hundred years from now, and with expressions of the hopes that humans in the next hundred years will find permanent peace and prosperity.

These are noble objectives—but, of course, they are not new. They are winning some public attention at this moment only because of the turn of the century. By the time you four young boys are out of college and taking your place in the adult world where decisions are made, the world will be well into the next century. The newness will have worn off, politicians will no longer be uttering their platitudes and others their prayers for the new millennium. Visions of a more civilized world will have faded as the people and their leaders find themselves too busy solving that day's problems and assuring their own futures to find much time to worry about the conditions of their neighbors, let alone the state of all humankind.

What I would hope for you, is that you never lose the vision, that wherever your education and your instincts and desires lead you in your vocations, you will never lose sight of the dream of a better world. I hope, of course, that your own lives are happy, peaceful, prosperous, and free from daily strife. But I also hope that if you achieve such success, you will keep forever in mind the millions less fortunate than yourselves, and

Letter to
My Grandchild

that you dedicate the intelligence I know that each of you possess and the knowledge I depend upon you to acquire, to better the world.

I hope you will avoid the terrible selfishness that has burdened most of the developed world in the last half of the century and that you will become leaders in seeking the improvement, first here at home and then around the world, that will truly set all humankind free to wipe forever from earth the scourge of war, ignorance, poverty, and pestilence.

Good luck and God bless your world of the twenty-first century.

Granddad

The Dalai Lama

TENZIN GYATSO WAS fifteen years old in 1950, when he was given the title of the fourteenth reincarnation of the Dalai Lama. By the time he was nineteen, he was negotiating with China's Mao Zedong over the future of Tibet, which China had invaded in 1950 and has occupied ever since. After years of failed peace talks and a violent suppression of Tibet's resistance movement, the Dalai Lama fled in 1959 to Dharmsala, India. As the leader of the Tibetan government-in-exile, the Dalai Lama has continued his efforts to promote peaceful solutions to international conflicts, and for this work he received the Nobel Peace Prize in 1989.

Dear Young Friends,

When we are strong, healthy and full of life, it is easy to forget that when we are born we are helpless. Throughout our early childhood we are entirely dependent on the kindness of others. By the time we reach our youth, we can look after ourselves and have few obligations. Consequently, we have some freedom and flexibility of thought and action. Perhaps this is why adults often say later that their younger years were the best time of their lives.

Because the future is open we feel free to do as we like. The important thing is to use this opportunity in a way that we will not later regret. Sooner or later we all acquire responsibilities that restrict our freedom. I am often surprised when I ask young people about their hopes for the future. Perhaps because it is so self-evident, very few reply simply that they want to be happy. But isn't it true, aren't all our plans based on a fundamental wish for happiness and contentment? However differently we may express it, as living beings what we all have in common is a wish from the very core of our being to be happy. Because it is of such prime importance, I think it is worth looking at how happiness can be brought about.

In general terms, both happiness and suffering can be divided broadly into two main categories, mental and physical. Of the two, our mental experience is the more powerful. For example, even if we have somehow hurt ourselves, say by painfully spraining an ankle, it does not prevent us from feeling happy when our friends come to visit us. On the other hand, if because of worry or disappointment we feel downhearted and miserable, even if we are offered our favourite food, we won't be able to enjoy it. So, it is useful to examine the causes of mental peace and happiness.

In my own limited experience, the basic source of all happiness is love and compassion, a sense of kindness and warmheartedness towards others. If you can be friendly and trusting towards others, you become more calm and relaxed. You lose the sense of fear and suspicion that we often feel about other people, either because we don't know them well or because we feel they are threatening or competing with us in some way. When you are calm and relaxed you can make proper use of your mind's ability to think clearly, so whatever you do, whether you are studying or working, you will be able to do it better.

Why should we be friendly and warmhearted towards other people? Because they are essentially just like us. Whether we are rich or poor, educated or uneducated, wherever we live and whether we belong to one nation, religion, culture or another, we are all just human beings. We are like brothers and sisters, members of one great human family. Like others we desire happiness and do not want suffering. Moreover, we all have an equal right to avoid suffering and seek happiness. This is why when I meet another person I try to think, "Here's another human being just like me, whose hopes and wishes are just like my own." Then friendly, kindhearted feelings arise of their own accord.

Everyone responds positively to kindness. One of the causes of the close bond between us and our parents is the natural kindness with which they take care of us. From the moment of conception in our mother's womb until we are able to look after ourselves we receive great kindness from many different people, without which we would not survive. Reflecting on this may inspire us to repay the kindness we have received by being kind to others ourselves.

Letter to
My Grandchild

We human beings are social creatures. We naturally seek friends and companionship and with few exceptions we dislike solitude. Now, what are the qualities that attract friends? Not anger, jealousy and deceit, but a kind concern for others, openness and sincerity.

As the twenty-first century approaches, our world is growing smaller and in many ways more friendly. However, we are also confronted by problems that affect us all, such as overpopulation, dwindling natural resources and an environmental crisis which threatens the very basis of our existence. There remains, besides, the difficulty of how to achieve genuine world peace. To meet the challenge of our times humanity must develop a greater sense of responsibility. Each of us must learn to work not just for our own self, family or nation, but for the benefit of all mankind. No one can afford to think that someone else will solve these problems. Each of us must really take his or her share of responsibility. Positive changes do not come quickly or easily, but I am hopeful.

I believe it is important that these issues do not merely remain the business of adults and that those of you who are still young should also be involved. The shape of the future is of even greater interest to you, who still have most of your lives before you. Even if only a few individuals try to create mental peace and happiness within themselves and act responsibly and kindheartedly towards others, they will have a positive influence in their community. And because of that I am confident that the coming century will see a more friendly, more caring and more understanding human family evolving on this planet.

With my good wishes and prayers,
Yours sincerely,
The Dalai Lama

**Umberto
Eco**

AUTHOR AND UNIVERSITY professor
Umberto Eco was born in Italy in 1929. He worked for Italian TV between 1954 and
1959 and subsequently served as a lecturer at several universities in Italy and the United
States. His novel *The Name of the Rose* achieved instant fame and attracted much critical
acclaim; it was made into a film in 1986. His later books include *Foucault's Pendulum.*

*Letter to
My Grandchild*

Dear Stefano,

Christmas is marching upon us, and soon the big stores downtown will be packed with excited fathers acting out their annual scenario of hypocritical generosity, having joyfully awaited this moment when they can buy for themselves—pretending it's for their sons—their cherished electric trains, the puppet theater, the target with bow and arrows, and the family Ping-Pong set. But I will still be an observer, because this year my turn hasn't yet come, you are too little, and Montessori-approved infant toys don't give me any great pleasure, probably because I don't enjoy sticking them in my mouth, even if the manufacturer's label assures me that they cannot be swallowed whole. No, I must wait, two years, or three or four. Then it will be my turn; the phase of mother-dominated education will pass, the rule of the teddy bear will decline and fall, and the moment will come when with the sweet and sacrosanct violence of paternal authority I can begin to mold your civic conscience. And then, Stefano . . .

  Then your presents will be guns. Double-barreled shotguns. Repeaters. Submachine guns. Cannons. Bazookas. Sabers. Armies of lead soldiers in full battle dress. Castles with drawbridges. Fortresses to besiege. Casemates, powder magazines, destroyers, jets. Machine guns, daggers, revolvers. Colts and Winchesters. Chassepots, 91's, Garands, shells, arquebuses, culverins, slingshots, crossbows, lead balls, catapults, firebrands, grenades, ballistas, swords, pikes, battering rams, halberds, and grappling hooks. And pieces of eight, just like Captain Flint's (in memory of Long John Silver and Ben Gun), and dirks, the kind that Don Barrejo so liked, and Toledo blades to knock aside three pistols at once and fell the Marquis of Montelimar, or using the Neapolitan feint with which the Baron de Sigognac slayed the evil ruffian who tried to steal his Isabelle. And there will be battle-axes, partisans, misericords, krises, javelins, scimitars, darts, and sword-sticks like the one John Carradine held when he was electrocuted on the third rail, and if nobody remembers that, it's their tough luck. And pirate cutlasses to make Carmaux and Van Stiller blanch, and damascened pistols like none Sir James Brook ever saw (otherwise he wouldn't have given up in the face of the sardonic, umpteenth cigarette of the Portuguese); and stilettos with triangular blades, like the one with which Sir William's disciple, as the day was gently dying at Clignancourt, killed the assassin Zampa, who killed his own mother, the old and sordid Fipart; and pères d'angoisse, like those inserted into the mouth of the jailer La Ramée while the Duke of Beaufort, the hairs of his coppery beard made even more fascinating thanks to the constant attention of a leaden comb, rode off, anticipating with joy the wrath of Mazarin; and muzzles loaded with nails, to be fired by men whose teeth are red with betel stains; and guns with mother-of-pearl stocks, to be grasped on Arab chargers with glistening coats; and lightning-fast bows, to turn the sheriff of Nottingham green with envy; and scalping knives, such as Minnehaha might have had, or (as you are bilingual) Winnetou. A small, flat pistol to tuck into a waistcoat under a frock coat, for the feats of a gentleman thief, or a ponderous Luger weighing down a pocket or filling an armpit à la Michael Shayne. And shotguns worthy of Jesse James and Wild Bill Hickok, or Sambigliong, muzzle-loading. In other words, weapons. Many weapons. These, my boy, will be the highlight of all your Christmases.

Sir, I am amazed—some will say—you, a member of a committee for nuclear disarmament and a supporter of the peace movement; you who join in marches on the capital and cultivate an Aldermaston mystique on occasion.

Do I contradict myself? Well, I contradict myself (as Walt Whitman put it).

One morning, when I had promised a present to a friend's son, I went into a department store in Frankfurt and asked for a nice revolver. Everyone looked at me, shocked. We do not carry warlike toys, sir. Enough to make your blood run cold. Mortified, I left, and ran straight into two Bundeswehr men who were passing on the sidewalk. I was brought back to reality. I wouldn't let anybody fool me. From now on I would rely solely on personal experience and to hell with pedagogues.

My childhood was chiefly if not exclusively bellicose. I used blowpipes improvised at the last minute among the bushes; I crouched behind the few parked cars, firing my repeater rifle; I led attacks with fixed bayonets. I was absorbed in extremely bloody battles. At home it was toy soldiers. Whole armies engaged in nerve-racking strategies, operations that went on for weeks, long campaigns in which I mobilized even the remains of my plush teddy bear and my sister's dolls. I organized bands of soldiers of fortune and made my few but faithful followers call me "the terror of Piazza Genova" (now Piazza Matteotti). I dissolved a group of Black Lions to merge with another, stronger outfit, then, once in it, I uttered a pronunciamento that proved disastrous. Resettled in the Monferrato area, I was recruited forcibly in the Band of the Road and was subjected to an initiation ceremony that consisted of a hundred kicks in the behind and a three-hour imprisonment in a chicken coop. We fought against the Band of Nizza Creek, who were filthy dirty and awesome. The first time, I took fright and ran off; the second time, a stone hit my lips, and I still have a little knot there I can feel with my tongue. (Then the real war arrived. The partisans let us hold their Stens for two seconds, and we saw some friends lying dead with a hole in their brow. But by now we were becoming adults, and we went along the banks of the Belbo River to catch the eighteen-year-olds making love, unless, in the grip of adolescent mystical crises, we had renounced all pleasures of the flesh.)

This orgy of war games produced a man who managed to do eighteen months of military service without touching a gun, devoting his long hours in the barracks to the grave study of medieval philosophy. A man of many iniquities but one who has always been innocent of the squalid crime of loving weapons and believing in the holiness and efficacy of warrior values. A man who appreciates an army only when he sees soldiers slogging through the muck after the Vajont disaster, engaged in a peaceful and noble civic purpose. A man who absolutely does not believe in just wars, who believes wars are unjust and damned and you fight always with reluctance, dragged into the conflict, hoping it will end quickly, and risking everything because it is a matter of honor and you can't evade it. I believe I owe my profound, systematic, cultivated, and documented horror of war to the healthy, innocent, platonically bloody releases granted me in childhood, just as when you leave a Western movie (after a furious brawl, the kind where the balcony of the saloon collapses, tables and big mirrors are broken, someone shoots at the piano player, and the plate-glass window shatters) cleaner, kinder, relaxed, ready to smile at the passerby who jostles you and to succor the sparrow fallen from its nest—as Aristotle was well aware, when he demanded of tragedy that it wave the blood-red flag before our eyes and purge us totally with the divine Epsom salts of catharsis.

Then I imagine the boyhood of Eichmann. Lying on his stomach, with that death's bookkeeper expression on his face as he studies the Meccano pieces and dutifully follows the instructions in the booklet; eager also to open the bright box of his new chemistry set; sadistic in laying out the tiny tools of the Little Carpenter, the plane the width of his hand and the twenty-centimeter saw, on a piece of plywood. Beware of boys who build miniature cranes! In their cold and distorted minds these little mathematicians are repressing the horrid complexes that will motivate their mature years. In every little monster who operates the switches of his toy railway lies a future director of death

Letter to
My Grandchild

camps! Watch out, if they are fond of those matchbox cars that the cynical toy industry produces for them, perfect facsimiles, with a trunk that really opens and windows that can be rolled up and down—terrifying! A terrifying pastime for the future commanders of an electronic army who, lacking all passions, will coldly press the red button of an atomic war!

You can identify them already. The big real-estate speculators, the slumlords who enforce evictions in the dead of winter; they have revealed their personality in the infamous game of Monopoly, becoming accustomed to the idea of buying and selling property and dealing relentlessly in stock portfolios. The Père Grandets of today, who have acquired with their mother's milk the taste for acquisition and learned insider trading with bingo cards. The bureaucrats of death trained on Lego blocks, the zombies of bureaucracy whose spiritual decease began with the rubber stamps and scales of the Little Post Office.

And tomorrow? What will develop from a childhood in which industrialized Christmases bring out American dolls that talk and sing and move, Japanese robots that jump and dance thanks to an inexhaustible battery, and radio-controlled automobiles whose mechanism will always be a mystery? . . .

Stefano, my boy, I will give you guns. Because a gun isn't a game. It is the inspiration for play. With it you will have to invent a situation, a series of relationships, a dialectic of events. You will have to shout boom, and you will discover that the game has only the value you give it, not what is built into it. As you imagine you are destroying enemies, you will be satisfying an ancestral impulse that boring civilization will never be able to extinguish, unless it turns you into a neurotic always taking Rorschach tests administered by the company psychologist. But you will find that destroying enemies is a convention of play, a game like so many others, and thus you will learn that it is outside reality, and as you play, you will be aware of the game's limits. You will work off anger and repressions, and then be ready to receive other messages, which contemplate neither death nor destruction. Indeed, it is important that death and destruction always appear to you as elements of fantasy, like Red Riding Hood's wolf, whom we all hated, to be sure, but without subsequently harboring an irrational hatred for Alsatians.

But this may not be the whole story, and I will not make it the whole story. I will not allow you to fire your Colts only for nervous release, in ludic purgation of primordial instincts, postponing until later, after catharsis, the *pars construens*, the communication of values. I will try to give you ideas while you are still hiding behind the armchair, shooting.

First of all, I will teach you to shoot not at the Indians but at the arms dealers and liquor salesmen who are destroying the Indian reservations. I will teach you to shoot at the Southern slave owners, to shoot in support of Lincoln. To shoot not at the Congo cannibals but at the ivory traders, and in a weak moment I may even teach you to stew Dr. Livingstone, I presume, in a big pot. We will play Arabs against Lawrence, and if we play ancient Romans, we'll be on the side of the Gauls, who were Celts like us Piedmontese and a lot cleaner than that Julius Caesar whom you will soon have to learn to regard with suspicion, because it is wrong to deprive a democratic community of its freedom, leaving as a tip, posthumously, gardens where the citizens can stroll. We'll be on the side of Sitting Bull against that repulsive General Custer. And on the side of the Boxers, naturally. With Fantomas rather than with Juve, who is too much a slave of duty to refuse, when required, to club an Algerian. But now I am joking: I will teach you, of

Letter to
My Grandchild

course, that Fantomas was a bad guy, but I won't tell you, not in complicity with the corrupt Baroness Orczy, that the Scarlet Pimpernel was a hero. He was a dirty Vendéen who caused trouble for the good guy Danton and the pure Robespierre, and if we play French Revolution, you'll participate in the taking of the Bastille.

These will be stupendous games. Imagine! And we'll play them together. Ah, so you wanted to let us eat cake, eh? All right, M. Santerre, let the drums roll! Tricoteuses of the world, unite and let your knitting needles do their worst! Today we'll play the beheading of Marie Antoinette!

You call this perverse pedagogy? And you, sir, antifascist practically since birth, have you ever played partisans with your son? Have you ever crouched behind the bed, pretending to be in the Langhe valleys, crying, Watch out, the Fascist Black Brigades are coming on the right! It's a roundup, they're shooting, return the Nazis' fire! No, you give your son building blocks and have the maid take him to some racist movie that glorifies the extinction of native Americans.

Dear Stefano, I will give you guns. And I will teach you to play extremely complicated wars, where the truth will never be entirely on one side. You will release a lot of energy in your young years, and your ideas may be a bit confused, but slowly you will develop some convictions. Then, when you are grown up, you will believe that it was all a fairy tale: little Red Riding Hood, Cinderella, the guns, the cannons, single combat, the witch and the seven dwarfs, armies against armies. But if by chance, when you are grown up, the monstrous characters of your childish dreams persist—witches, trolls, armies, bombs, compulsory military service—perhaps, having gained a critical attitude toward fairy tales, you will learn to live and criticize reality.

Umberto Eco

Oriana Fallaci

WRITER AND JOURNALIST Oriana Fallaci was born in 1930 in Italy. In 1946, she received her first assignment as a journalist. She began working as a correspondent in 1950, and starting in 1967 served as a war correspondent in the Middle East, Vietnam, Pakistan, and South America.

Oriana Fallaci's books include *A Man* and *Inshallah.* She has won several international prizes, including the Hemingway Prize for Literature.

Letter to
My Grandchild

Will you be a man or a woman? I would like you to be a woman, my child, because I don't agree at all with my mother, who thinks that being born a woman is a misfortune and always moans: "Oh, if only I had been born a man!" Yes, I know, ours is a world which was fabricated by men for men: man's dictatorship is so rooted that it extends even to the language. We say "men" to say men and women, "man-day" to indicate the working day of a man or a woman, "man-made" to point out an object made by a man or a woman, "mankind" to refer to the human race, "manhood" to refer to courage, "manslaughter" to refer to killing. And in the legend that men invented to explain life the first creature is not a woman. It is a man named Adam. Eve arrives later, to amuse him and to bring him troubles. In the paintings which adorn our churches, God is an old man with a white beard. Never an old woman with white hair. And all their heroes are men from that Prometheus who discovered fire to that Icarus who tried to fly, up to that Jesus who is called Son of the Father and of the Holy Spirit as if his mother were an incubator or a wet-nurse. Yet, or just because of that, being a woman is so enchanting: an adventure which requires such a courage, a challenge that never bores. You will have so many things to undertake if you are born a woman, my child. To begin with, you will have to fight in order to demonstrate that if God existed it could be an old woman or a beautiful girl. Then you will have to fight to demonstrate that sin did not start when

Eve picked the apple: rather than sin, that day she originated a splendid virtue called disobedience. Finally, you will have to fight to prove that inside your body there is an intelligence which screams to be heard. Being a mother is not a duty, it is a right among many rights. You'll get so tired of repeating it. And often, almost always, you will lose. But woe to you if you feel discouraged. Fighting is much more beautiful than winning, remember, travelling is much more amusing than arriving. When you arrive or you win, you sense such a void. To overcome that void you must start a new journey, create a new goal, and yes: I do hope that you will be a woman.

But if you will be a man, I will be just as happy. And maybe a little happier because you will be spared so many humiliations, so many servitudes, so many abuses. You will not have to fear a rape in the dark of a street, for instance, you will not have to use a nice face to be accepted, a nice body to hide your brain. You will not have to hear that sin originated by your picking an apple. And you'll feel much less tired, you'll be able to disobey without being scorned, to defend yourself without being insulted. . . . But look out, my child, look out: you also will have to bear other slaveries, other injustices. Not even for a man life is easy. As you will have stronger muscles, they will ask you to carry heavier loads; they will impose upon you heavier tasks. As you will have a beard, they will laugh at you if you cry or search for tenderness. As you will have a tail on your

Letter to
My Grandchild

groin, a penis, they will order you to kill and get killed in war. They will demand your complicity to continue the male tyranny they started in the caves. Yet, or just because of that, being a man will be such a beautiful enterprise: a challenge which will never bore you. Or I hope so because, if you will be a man, I hope that you will be the man I always dreamed: sweet with the weak, ferocious with the arrogant, generous with those who love you, pitiless with those who command you, enemy of anyone who tells you that Jesus is the son of a father and of a holy spirit not of the woman who gave him birth. My dear child, I am trying to explain to you that being a man does not mean having a tail on your groin: a penis. It means being a person. And above all I want you to be a person. It is a marvellous word, the word person, because it does not put limits to the words man and woman. It does not mark frontiers between those who have a tail on their groin and those who don't. Besides, the thread which divides those who have the tail from those who don't is so thin. Heart and brain have no sex. Nor does behaviour. If you will be a person of heart and brain, remember, I will not ask you to behave in one way or another because you are male or female. I will only ask you to exploit well the miracle of being born and never, never, never surrender to cowardice.

Oriana Fallaci

**Marilyn
French**

WRITER AND CRITIC Marilyn French was born in 1929 in the United States. She is the author of the feminist classic *The Women's Room,* as well as *The Bleeding Heart* and *Our Father.*

*Letter to
My Grandchild*

Dear One,

Having no grandchild, I address all the children being born today and in days to come. Like all of us, you enter a world you never made. If you are lucky, your family will make it sweet and safe for you for many years. If you are unlucky, you may discover the world's harshness when you are too young to deal with it. But in either case, you will experience sorrow and loss in your young years, because we all do.

It is customary to address the young in sweet tones, to pretend that life can be without pain or sorrow, and to speak only of the beautiful and kind. But doing this leaves a child unprepared for much of what all children experience. I disliked being lied to as a child, and I will not lie to you. The world outside, as well as the world within the family, can be cruel and harsh. All of us need to be able to perceive this, and at the same time cherish the people and events and objects that make the world rich and colorful and joyous. It is important to learn to cherish the beauty and worth of all human beings, of animals, and of the planet we inhabit.

Life has built-in sorrow because we die, and what is worse, people we love also die. But humans make life far harsher than it needs to be, because of a disease that has been rampant in the world for several thousand years, a disease called power-worship. This illness has only recently been diagnosed under this name. It is so old that many people revere it; they do not see it as an illness, but as a good. They exalt the rewards it can bring, much as the devil exalted the knowledge and power he wanted to trade for the soul of a scholar, Faustus, in an old tale. Those who worship power point to riches, to the awe and jealousy of other people, and to a sense of personal importance as the highest goods the world has to offer. They will tell you that all worthy people desire these goods.

I hope you will not believe them. There are real goods on earth, but they do not lie in power. These are the goods cherished by the healers, those who work to end the power-disease. Healers are permitted to glimpse the promised land; they are able to feel joy and the pleasures of sharing and love and community and friendship. The sick ones are unable to feel these pleasures; they have forsaken their souls. They try to gather what the world calls goods—money, objects, and power. They amass so much they cannot use all of what they have, yet they keep trying to amass more and more. In their blind greed, they seem to want no one else to have anything. They deprive so many others that they must hire men with guns or live in fortresses, to protect them and their possessions from being stolen. They live in fear and anxiety. They can trust no one: they suspect even those intimates they share with. Suspecting love, they deny it.

But healers see through this false religion, this worship of the meretricious. They understand that the true goods in life—once basic needs are met—produce pleasure. Healers find work they enjoy and take satisfaction in. Often their work involves assisting others. Healers have beloved friends with whom they celebrate mutuality, enlarging their circles with love. They approach life with delight. When overcome by grief—which comes to everyone—they can be consoled by the embraces of their loved ones: intimates, family, and friends.

Healers cannot simply live their lives in pleasure, though, ignoring the sick. It will take some time to heal this disease, and they must help fight it. For the diseased want to possess *everything!* They want to deprive others of even basic needs—food, housing, clothing, medical care, education. They believe that if they *can* seize all the world's material goods, they have the right to do so. In fact, they believe that those who do not devote themselves to amassing money and power are inferior beings—for they think that amassing power constitutes the meaning of life. Healers must struggle with them in whatever way they can, so that they do not seize all the world's goods and impoverish all the rest of the world's people. Healers must struggle with them for the souls of the children, and the bodies of the poor. Healers can help them to recognize their disease; they can rescue their victims; they can create delight and interest through the arts or athletics or intellectual practice. Whatever course they take, they are doubly blessed: they are helping to cure a sickness; and they are building felicitous life for themselves.

So my wish for you is that you gain the wisdom and grace to choose a life of healing and pleasure.

Marilyn French

Jostein Gaarder

JOSTEIN GAARDER, BORN in 1952 in Norway, has taught philosophy for many years. The novel *Sophie's World* was his first book to appear in English and has been a best-seller in over forty countries. Other of his books include *The Solitaire Mystery*, *The Christmas Mystery*, and *That Same Flower*.

Letter to
My Grandchild

On Wednesday, April 10th, 1912, the *Titanic* set out from Southampton, England, on her maiden voyage to New York. Four days later, after running into an iceberg, the luxury liner sank and 1,500 people drowned in the freezing water.

The *Titanic* was built at a time characterized by technological advance and the belief that man would, once and for all, gain ascendancy over nature. This liner—the largest passenger ship in the world and the new jewel in the crown of British shipping—was regarded as a great triumph for technology. With all of its watertight bulkheads the *Titanic* was an "unsinkable ship."

The crossing itself was marked by the same air of human presumption. The captain ignored six iceberg warnings and sailed full steam ahead, at a speed of 21 knots. The telegraph operator on board also neglected to acknowledge the liner *California*'s warnings of icebergs in the shipping lanes. He had enough to do, sending greetings to family and friends ashore. Nonetheless, at a quarter past midnight on April 15th, 1912, he was forced to send out an SOS: the first time in history that this distress signal had ever been sent. SOS.

Even when the ship is struck by an iceberg both crew and passengers treat this occurrence with the greatest unconcern. Many of those who are still awake rush gleefully on deck to watch the iceberg slip past. They pluck chunks of ice from the berg and pop them in their drinks. Some raise their glasses and drink a toast to the British Empire. The collision with the iceberg is seen as a bit of a diversion on the long crossing.

Some hours later, grim panic reigns on board the ship—which has lifeboat spaces for no more than half of the passengers. But once the last lifeboat has been lowered into the water a strange calm settles over the *Titanic*. The alarm and confusion are past and hundreds of people are left standing on the top deck.

The great majority of those who went down with the *Titanic* were travelling third-class. And here, too, it was the wealthiest who were best able to save themselves. Not only was the ship fitted with watertight bulkheads, the companionway leading from the third-class cabins to the lifeboats was blocked off. Even so, there were those who managed to battle their way up on deck, but by then the last lifeboat had been launched.

* * *

"*Titanic!* The vessel's name testifies to a fatal irony. It took its name from the Titans of Greek mythology, who were known for their overweening confidence, their hubris and recklessness. In the end, the Titans challenged the gods on Olympia—and were hurled down into the underworld.

The story also goes that a number of prophecies were made about the sinking of the *Titanic*. There had been no shortage of warnings. The most curious example of these is the book *Futility*, published 14 years before the *Titanic* went down. It tells of the sinking of a massive holiday steamer, the *Titan*. In all aspects—from the ship's tonnage, the technical details and number of passengers to the actual course of events—so closely does this resemble the sinking of the *Titanic* that it quite takes the reader's breath away. Both in the book and in the reality of 14 years later the disaster occurred while crossing the Atlantic Ocean, in April, due to collision with an iceberg, at a speed of over 20 knots and with few survivors. The author, Morgan Robertson, maintained that the story of the *Titan* had been passed to him by a voice inside his head.

The loss of the *Titanic* will stand for all time as a symbol of the arrogance of mankind, of our unwavering conviction that "everything will be fine"—or that "the captain must know what he's doing." After all, could the earth not be likened to one great vessel, with all of us in the same boat? Though in our own day it might be more appropriate to compare the earth to a spaceship.

Being an astronaut tends to bring out the ecologist in one. Innumerable astronauts have described how, from space, they perceived the earth as a living entity—as an organism, even. One of these, Jack Robert Lousma, describes the experience with these words: "You don't see the borders between countries when you're orbiting the earth in a space shuttle. Up there it's possible to imagine—and hope—that there will come a time, down here, when we will be able to live without borders cutting off people from one another. Like *Columbia*, the earth is a kind of space shuttle travelling through space. Both have limited resources. Maybe sometime we will be able to agree on how best to make use of these."

"Spaceship Earth is in big trouble" is how another astronaut put it. "But the situation is not hopeless. We can overcome the present crisis and ensure that humanity has a pleasant spaceflight. We can do it—provided that we radically alter the way in which we treat our fellow passengers and our ship."

From outer space, the cities of the earth show up as unsightly scars. Motorways fan out from the cities in all directions. And new cities spring up. . . .

It has been said that "the problem with spaceship Earth is that we were never issued with an owner's manual." But that is no longer the case. We know that we are on a collision course with nature. We know that we have to reduce our speed and we know in which direction our new course should take us. And yet: are we not taking our situation as lightly as the passengers on the *Titanic* took the first reports of the iceberg?

"You must love your neighbour as yourself, because you are your neighbour," said India's former president Radhakrishnan "It is an illusion that leads you to think that your neighbour is anyone other than yourself."

Is it perhaps also an illusion to think that this earth is anything other than myself?

Jostein Gaarder

Nadine Gordimer

WRITER NADINE GORDIMER was born in 1923 in South Africa. She has been politically active most of her life, and has often written about the tensions between white radicals, liberals, and blacks in her homeland. Her most widely read books are *The Conservationist* and *Burger's Daughter.* She received the Booker Prize for *The Conservationist* in 1974 and the Nobel Prize for Literature in 1991. She was vice president for PEN's international department in 1987 and has been a member of the African National Congress since 1990.

Letter to
My Grandchild

Dearest Pascale,

I address this letter to you because you were my firstborn grandchild and therefore marked a special occasion and a new phase in the progress of my own life, although much of whatever I have to say to you belongs also to your sister Paule and your cousins Kate and Roland.

Nevertheless, I do want to say to you that my pleasure at meeting you for the first time when you were about two months old was only the beginning of the fun and joy I have had in the loving friendship that has grown up between us when we have visited one another—granny and young woman—between your parents' home in France and mine in South Africa, over twenty years.

I'm not much of one for giving advice about *How to Live.* I've made my own mistakes, and you will make yours, whatever any of us tells you to do or warns you not to do, since the specific circumstances of each life and time and place often require different responses. I can only hope fervently for you that your life will be lived in a society without internal strife, political or religious intolerance, and in a world without wars. Of course, that is too much to ask for; alas, it seems, looking back at this century, that there will always be wars going on somewhere. Selfishly, I have to say that I want you to be safe from them, but also that you should understand and take your individual share of the responsibility of thinking clearly about the causes of conflict and supporting all and every means of promoting peace. You may say: what can an individual do, in comparison with the powers that make international decisions for us? Tolerance, in your relations at home and with your friends and workmates, tolerance of the differences within your own society, recognition that we are all human and vulnerable under the skin, no matter what colour that skin is, that we all want to live with dignity, based on the same needs, material and emotional—that is the foundation of the tolerance that could create peace in our world.

You're going to mature in a new century. My wish for you is that you may find the reward of satisfaction in doing work that you give your best to and enjoy; that your bright-eyed enthusiasm for new experiences and new sights may never desert your spirit, and that you will love and be loved.

As we say in South Africa, *Hamba kahle*. Go well.

Love,

Your Ouma,
Nadine Gordimer

Katharine Graham

WRITER AND PUBLISHER Katharine Graham was born in New York City in 1917 and graduated from the University of Chicago in 1938. She worked as a reporter for the *San Francisco News* before she joined the staff of the *Washington Post*, which her father, Eugene Meyer, had purchased in 1933. Her husband, Philip Graham, became its publisher from 1946 until his death in 1963. Mrs. Graham took over the helm of the company upon his death, holding various top-ranking positions. She is now chairman of the executive committee.

Katharine Graham is the author of the Pulitzer Prize–winning memoir *Personal History.*

Dear Grandchildren—

You stretch over a period of thirty-one years. In many ways, it is impossible for us in my generation to say much that would be helpful to each of you in yours. The world we have come through is vastly different from the one you are now in and which still awaits you. You do even now, and will in the future, live in a world made even smaller and brought ever closer by still undreamed of technologies; a world characterized more by intranational turmoil than by the bipolar conflicts of the Cold War world; a world of immense economic challenges on global and individual levels; and a world of different mores, customs, and traditions.

My hopes for you are many, beginning with the hope that some of the qualities and characteristics from the world I have known will endure and that you will help to carry these on and even strengthen them.

I hope that you live in a world at peace, one where nuclear weapons are controlled and nuclear energy is used productively; that you live in a world in which you can trust and believe in each other, one where families are strong and thriving, with parents nurturing and supporting children in every possible way; that you live in a world with established educational goals here and in places where they hardly now exist, where the drive is to educate all of humanity and each human being to his or her full potential; and that you live in a world with greater economic equality and more widespread social justice.

I hope some form of democracy, whether constitutional or parliamentary, survives and thrives, and that freedom—or even the four Freedoms with which Franklin Roosevelt once inspired our world—lives and flourishes.

Above all, I hope you develop and retain your own high-minded goals, while having a good time, a lot of laughs, personal friendships, and love along the way.

Katharine Graham

Václav Havel

WRITER AND POLITICIAN Václav Havel was born in 1936 in Czechoslovakia. Regarded as the foremost pioneer of the modern absurdist stage play in his homeland, Havel also helped found the human rights group Charta 77. Although frequently faced with imprisonment and house arrest, he was elected president of the Czech and Slovak Federal Republic in 1989, and since 1993 has been president of the Czech Republic. His plays include *The Memorandum* and *The Increased Difficulty of Concentration.* His books include *Letters to Olga* and *Disturbing the Peace.*

*Letter to
My Grandchild*

The Hindus have a legend concerning a mythical bird called Bherunda. The bird had a single body, but two necks, two heads, and two separate consciousnesses. After an eternity together, these two heads began to hate each other and decided to harm each other. Both of them swallowed pebbles and poison, and the result was predictable; the whole Bherunda bird went into spasms and died with loud cries of pain. It was brought back to life by the infinite mercy of Krishna, to remind people forever how all hatred ends up.

We should remind ourselves of this legend each day. For as soon as one of us succumbs to the temptation to hate another, we will all end up like the Bherunda bird.

A thousand times over the past decades I have seen backs in my country bent allegedly in the interest of children. A thousand times I have heard people defend their servitude to a hated regime by arguing that they were only doing it for their children: so they could feed them, make it possible for them to study, to afford seaside vacations for them. A thousand times, both acquaintances and strangers have confided to me that they were heart, mind, and soul totally on our side, but that they signed various petition campaigns aimed against us, and organized by the totalitarian government, for the sole reason that they had children and thus could not afford the luxury of resistance. Immorality was committed in the name of children, and evil was served for their alleged good.

I have experienced a beautiful revolt of children against the lie that their parents had served, allegedly in the interest of those very children. Our antitotalitarian revolution was—at least in its beginnings—a children's revolution. It was high school students and apprentices, adolescents, who marched in the streets. They marched when their parents were still afraid, were afraid for their children and for themselves. They locked their children in at home, took them away from the cities on weekends. Then they started marching in the streets with them. First out of fear for their children, later because they became infected by their enthusiasm. The children evoked from their parents their better selves. They convinced them they were lying and forced them to take a stand on the side of truth.

And what about the children of dissidents? Although they could not study and had to endure the arrests and persecutions of their parents, they did not blame them but instead respected them. They were more interested in a moral example than in the advantages stemming from a bent back.

Children in our country have proven that the ideology of sacrificing truth for the alleged interest of children is false. They revolted against parents who advocated this ideology, they joined the few who had been convinced from the very beginning that they would serve their children best if they did not look for excuses and lie, but rather live in truth and thus give an example to their children.

The international community has achieved something unprecedented. Most of the countries of the world have, within months, joined an exceptionally good, precise, and exhaustive international agreement for the protection of children. I rejoice, as we all do, in this achievement and am proud that I had the honor of signing the agreement on behalf of my country this morning.

At the same time, however, I believe that this agreement—or any other conceivable international document—cannot protect children from pseudo-protection, that is, from

Letter to
My Grandchild

their parents committing more evil in the name and in the interest of children—whether in good faith, in self-delusion, or by deliberately lying—and from hurting themselves more than they can hurt the children.

As with any law, this one too can only acquire real meaning and significance if it is accompanied by real moral self-awareness, by which I mean the moral self-awareness of parents.

You cannot put that into a law. However, if it were possible, I would add another paragraph to the agreement I signed this morning. This paragraph would say that it is forbidden for parents and adults in general in the name and allegedly in the interest of children, to lie, serve dictatorships, inform, bend their back, be afraid of tyrants, and betray their friends and ideals. And that it is forbidden for all murderers and dictators to pat children on the head.

Václav Havel

Thor Heyerdahl

ZOOLOGIST, ANTHROPOLOGIST, AND author Thor Heyerdahl was born in 1914 in Norway. He was leader of the 1947 Kon-Tiki expedition, a journey he repeated in 1970 when he crossed the Atlantic in a re-created prehistoric boat, setting out to prove that the Peruvian Indians could have settled in Polynesia. He then returned to South America to study the pyramids of the Tucume. Heyerdahl's expeditions have been documented in book form as well as on film, the Kon-Tiki documentary winning an Oscar in 1951.

These expeditions, however, are only the dramatic peaks in a long, continuous, and unorthodox scientific career that has won Thor Heyerdahl numerous prizes and honorary titles.

My dear Grandchildren,

I send you this letter stamped and posted as surface mail, so you can save it for your children as a souvenir from a period when man used ink and envelopes with stamps, and had handwritten messages mailed and delivered to your door by postmen. We invented the telefax and CD-ROM discs, you may invent an electronic time-and-space eliminator, so please transfer my advice to a system your children can understand before man forgets to read and write.

My testament to my heirs is some advice:

Take care of what is left of nature. Venerate the green environment and mighty unseen behind it that evolved all life. We did not during our generation.

Forgive us for the forests we have depleted. For the ocean we have polluted. For the holes we have torn in the ozone layers. Our parents in their ignorance told us to struggle for progress. We misinterpreted the word. We thought progress meant to combat nature. To free mankind from the ties to the human past. To give our descendants a better life in a man-made world.

The Churches, the Synagogues, the Mosques told us that nature was a product of God who rested on his seventh day proud of his work. But one day for God is a thousand for men. And Darwin scared us with the picture of apeman behind us.

Bewildered, we assaulted what we considered a wilderness. Declared unlimited war against our own environment with bulldozers and spray bottles. But we rested on the seventh day as God said. Not the Seventh Day of God but the seventh day of man. That meant Sundays for the Christians, Saturdays for the Jews, and Fridays for the Moslems. The rest of the weeks, the years, the millennia for man, we built city walls between us and our original environment. The natural environment that alone had bred us and fed us according to Darwin. That was donated to us by its creator, according to those who trusted God. We have narrowed our horizons with city walls and blinded our view of the heavenly bodies by neon lights.

We have worshipped dead things. Gold and robots. You must worship the spirit of life in all that grows and moves.

We thought progress meant better weapons to enforce peace on our enemies on our own terms. But experience has shown us that whether we invent bow and arrow or nuclear bombs, the enemy copies our weapons and turns them against us. We have built machinery to free laborers from heavy work, but the machinery took over the industry and sent the laborers unemployed into the streets. We have invented computers and hundreds of ingenious devices to save time and spend the time saved working to pay our bills. So we have ended up more stressed and more confused than any generation before us.

We have been looking down upon indigenous people. They believe there is something natural and yet superhuman that pushes colorful flowers up from the black soil, that unfolds tender leaves through dry bark. Indigenous tribes had no microscopes, like we have, to see the chromosomes and genes which are programmed to follow the laws of nature. You, my heirs, try to see behind what we see, like they did.

As we do today, you may wonder forever why you are born and what the purpose of life may be. We thought it was to rebuild the world around us, and have tried. You may have better success if you try to adjust and repair the world inside you. The eternal and infinite universe is inside us. On the blind side of our eyes.

Letter to
My Grandchild

Forgive us and our parents for not understanding how well Darwin's theory of creation through evolution follows the chronology split up into human days by the sages in Antiquity when they wrote the parable about Genesis. Read either version at your own pick, and you will understand that all that walk and fly came after all that crawl and swim, and all are members of our extended family.

And so and also all those who can neither see nor hear and are stuck on roots in the ground, moving up so slowly that we do not see it and think them motionless and dead even though they change from day to day. All that live on this planet are our relatives. For we have all inherited life from our common ancestors, the single-celled plankton that began evolution of all life on Earth. All life has a single origin. A common beginning, whether formed by supernatural creation or by natural evolution. Even evolution, before it began, must have had an input, something creative to set it going in a sensible direction. If nature created its own evolution, then it is worthy of respect and veneration as our own superior. If there is a spirit of God in all life that grew out of a sterile sea and a virgin soil, then respect and venerate his work which is our environment, and worship your God under any name that fits your faith and your language.

Thor Heyerdahl, Ph.D.

Doris Lessing

WRITER DORIS LESSING was born in Iran in 1919 and grew up in Southern Rhodesia (now Zimbabwe). Her first published novel was *The Grass Is Singing*, a study of white civilization in Africa, the theme of many of her early works. Notable examples of her work are the five-volume sequence *Children of Violence* and *The Golden Notebook*.

Letter to My Grandchild

I have a problem: I have *two* grandchildren. . . .

There is, these days, an agenda of possible disasters in store for the human race, and we are all familiar with thoughts about pollution, soil erosion, the poisoning of the seas, the disappearance of the forests, radioactivity, and so on.

This week there has been a new and nasty addition to our list of woes. We have read that scientists think the Gulf Stream may be weakening. This may be the beginning of something worse. Their researches into ice cores prove that changes in climate, as drastic as those which usher in ice ages, or end them, are not slow and almost imperceptible, but can happen suddenly, in as little as ten years. The suggestion is that all of our civilisations, the product of our known history—the story of our last ten thousand years—are the result of a quite unusual world climate. And that everything we depend on may vanish—quite quickly, and quite soon. *May*—we do not know. Human beings are very good at coping with disasters and sudden change—we have survived mass epidemics, disastrous wars, climate changes, famines, floods, fires, genocide—there is no end to our courage and adaptability. And now—possibly—all our qualities are going to be tested to their limit. And I have every faith in you and your generation.

Doris Lessing

Astrid
Lindgren

WRITER ASTRID LINDGREN was born in 1907 in Sweden. She is the author of a vast number of children's books and is best known for *Pippi Longstocking,* a groundbreaking story which abandoned the traditional moralizing undertones in children's literature. Several of her books have been dramatized, and she is the winner of many literary awards. Since the 1980s, Astrid Lindgren has also played an important political role in the protection of children and animals.

SUSY SPRY

I wish you could see the house where Susy Spry lived! It was so neat and small you could almost believe that it was some kind of fairytale house with dwarves and elves living in it.

The house sat on a small steep street of cobbled stones in the very poorest part of town. It was a really poor street and none of the other houses in the street were any grander than Susy Spry's house.

Susy Spry's house! What am I saying? Of course it wasn't Susy who owned the house; it was Gran, Gran who made polka-pigs that she sold at the market on Saturdays—what are polka-pigs? They're those peppermint flavoured sweets with red and white stripes on them. Very good they are too! And polka-pigs are what they're called in Sweden where Susy lived. Now, as I said before, the house was actually Gran's. But I call it Susy Spry's house anyway.

Susy could usually be found sitting on the front door steps when you passed her house. She had the brownest and most cheerful eyes and the reddest cheeks ever seen on a child, and she looked so—how shall I put it?—she looked so spry. Yes, that's it, "spry"! And that was exactly why her grandmother had started calling her Susy Spry in the first place. Gran said that Susy Spry had looked spry even when she was only three months old and lay in a basket that someone delivered at Gran's with a note telling her to take care of the child, "because no one else is going to."

Oh, how snug it was, that little house! Two small windows facing the street; and behind them you would often glimpse a small nose and two cheerful brown eyes. Behind the house, well hidden behind a tall green fence, was a small garden, that is if you can call it a garden at all; the whole thing was nothing but a cherry tree and some gooseberry bushes. Well, then there was the tiny patch of green grass too. And that's where Gran and Susy used to sit and drink their coffee in the spring sunshine on a fine day. Actually, it was Gran who did the coffee drinking. Susy just dipped lumps of sugar in Gran's coffee. And then she would throw bread crumbs to the sparrows frolicking on the garden path right next to the border of snowdrops.

In Susy's opinion, Gran's house was just grand, even though it was so small. In the evenings, when she got into her bed in the kitchen bench, with Gran sitting at the table cutting papers for her sweets, she would say her prayers in a loud and clear voice:

An angel with two candles bright
Walks outside our house at night
A great book in his hands he keeps
Now I lay me down to sleep.

Susy was very happy about that angel walking outside their house at night. It felt somehow reassuring. It was just that she was a bit worried about how he managed to carry all those things: two bright candles, and a book. She would dearly have liked to see how he did it—and how did he get over the fence? Maybe someday she would manage to catch a glimpse of the angel. Up to now, she hadn't had much luck. He must be doing all his walking about while Susy slept.

When what I am about to tell you now happened, Susy wasn't seven years old yet. There was nothing mysterious about what happened. Gran slid on the kitchen floor and hurt her leg. Nothing more mysterious than that and such things happen every single day; but just think that there was only one week left before Christmas! Just think of all the peppermint polka-pigs that needed selling at the great Christmas market. Who would do that now that Gran was tied up in bed and couldn't move her leg without almost crying out loud? Who would cook the Christmas ham and buy the Christmas presents and make all the Christmas preparations in the house?

"I will!" said Susy—I already told you that she was a spry sort of girl.

"Oyoyoy," said Gran from her bed. "Sweet child, you can't do that. We must ask Mrs. Larsson if she will take you in for Christmas and then we must hear if I can get into the hospital."

Then Susy looked more spry than ever. Was she to stay with the Larssons? Was Gran going to be at the hospital? Weren't Gran and Susy going to celebrate Christmas together like they used to do? Oh yes, they most certainly were! said Susy—almost seven and with the brownest and most cheerful eyes in the world.

And then she threw herself into the Christmas cleaning. First, she had to ask Gran: "How do you go about it, Christmas cleaning?" Susy had only a vague idea that one turned the entire house upside down leaving the furniture topsy-turvy and everything as cheerless as possible. Then one put everything back in place—and then Christmas came.

Gran said that they needn't be so particular this year. "We'll just skip the window cleaning." But Susy wouldn't hear of it. Really, one couldn't celebrate Christmas without clean curtains. And one definitely couldn't put up the fresh curtains if the windows were grimy.

Mrs. Larsson did come over and helped a bit—that she did. She scrubbed the floors in the small kitchen and in the small room; that was all the room there was. She also cleaned the windows. But apart from that, Susy did everything herself. You should have seen her as she bustled about with a kerchief tied around her head and a rag in her hand. She looked spryer than spry can be. She hung the fresh curtains. She spread the rag mats on the kitchen floor and dusted all the furniture. And in the middle of everything, she had to make Gran coffee and fry sausage and potatoes. She had to light the stove all by herself. Lucky thing it was such a good stove. Susy fed it kindling wood and crumpled-up newspaper and blew, and then she listened eagerly for it to start crackling. Yes, there it went now, crackling! Gran got her coffee and she wagged her head and said,

"Bless your heart, dear sweet child, how would I get along without you?"

And Susy sat on the edge of the bed with a big smear of black soot on her nose and dipped a lump of sugar into Gran's coffee before going back to her cleaning.

But then, how about the polka-pigs that were already boiled and ready for selling at the market? Who would do that? Susy Spry and no one else—even though Susy didn't really know how to reckon yet or to weigh off sweets on the small scales as Gran used to do at her sweet stall at the market. But Susy knew how a 50-oere coin looked—and no mistake about it. Gran had to sit up in bed and weigh polka-pigs into bags. Three and a half ounces in each bag. That would make it 50 oere each.

The Christmas market was three days before Christmas. That morning, Susy was up early and served Gran breakfast in bed.

"Dear sweet child!" said Gran. "It's so cold. You'll freeze your nose off."

Susy just laughed. She was all ready for her great exciting polka-pig adventure. And how she was wrapped up! Two thick sweaters under her coat and her cap pulled well down over her ears and a woolen scarf around her neck and big red mittens and then Gran's colossal rush shoes to protect her toes from getting frostbitten—and slung over her arm the basket filled with polka-pigs.

"Bye now, Gran," Susy said and hurried out into the winter gloom. Already the streets were busy with people. Well, I should think so—after all it was Christmas market day! It was bitterly cold. The snow creaked under Gran's rush shoes while Susy made her way to the market square. But soon the sky started to colour prettily in the east. It looked like a fine day ahead. Larsson had been kind enough to put up Gran's stall in its usual place at the market square. So, all Susy had to do was to arrange the polka-pigs in neat rows. The other market women gaped at her.

"Has Mathilda taken complete leave of her senses?! Really, she can't let that child stand at the stall!" they said.

"Well, that's exactly what she's going to do." said Susy Spry. Her breath steamed from her mouth like smoke and her brown eyes sparkled with eagerness as she arranged her sweets.

"If that isn't the tiniest little market vendor I've ever seen!" said the mayor as he passed on his way to the town hall. And then he bought two bags of polka-pigs and handed Susy a shiny 1-krona coin.

"Oh no!" Susy said. "I need two coins. Two 50-oere, that's what I must have."

The mayor laughed and fished out two 50-oere coins. "Here you go," he said. "And you can keep the krona too, you spry little rascal."

But Susy wouldn't. "No, I need two 50-oere," she said. "One for each bag. That's what Gran said."

Susy's stall had many customers. Everyone wanted to buy from the tiniest little vendor at the market. But then Gran's polka-pigs were the best in town, red and white and sweet and lovely. Susy had a cigar box for the money and more and more coins piled up in it. But only 50-oere coins. Susy would accept nothing else.

The other market women were feeling the first pangs of envy as they watched the roaring business Susy was doing. Susy herself was so happy and excited that she almost couldn't keep still. Oh, she was going to make a great trade out of this. She was going to boil sweets by the million and go to the market square every single day!

Gran lay at home in her bed and was just napping a little when Susy came rushing in and emptied the contents of her cigar box onto the covers. And the basket was empty—not a single polka-pig left.

"Bless your heart, dear sweet child," said Gran as usual. "How would I get along without you?"

But how about the Christmas presents, then? Now, Gran hadn't been able to buy anything beforehand. She had wanted to wait till after the Christmas market because they didn't have any money until then. But here she lay now and couldn't move. And Susy who had her heart set on a doll—not just any doll. Oh no, the most wonderful doll in the world from Söderlund's store on Church Street. Gran and Susy had looked at it many times and Gran had secretly asked Miss Söderlund to hold the doll till after the Christmas market. The doll wore a white lace dress and could open and close her eyes and was, all in all, the prettiest doll that money could buy.

But then Gran couldn't possibly send Susy to buy her own Christmas present, could she? Oh yes, nothing else for it. But what a clever plan they cooked up, Gran and Susy. Gran wrote a note to Miss Söderlund—a secret note. "SECRET!" it read on it. Maybe that was unnecessary really, because in any case Susy couldn't read. Clutching the note, Susy ran along to Söderlund's. Miss Söderlund studied the note long and carefully. And then Susy had to go into the back room of the store where that strange smell was. When she had been sitting there for a while, Miss Söderlund came in and gave her a big parcel, saying, "Now, you go straight home to Gran with this—and mind you don't drop the parcel!"

Oh no, Susy didn't drop the parcel. She just felt it a little. She was hoping that it was the doll but there was no way of knowing really. Susy bought a present for Gran also: a lovely pair of knitted gloves that Gran had wanted for a long time.

Did anyone believe that Christmas would never come around at Susy Spry and her Gran's? Then I suggest they should have looked in through one of the small windows on that Christmas Eve. That's when they would have seen the fresh curtains, the rag mats on the floor, and the fine Christmas tree right next to Gran's bed. Susy had bought it herself at the market and decorated it with candles and flags and apples and polka-pigs. They would also have seen Susy sitting on the edge of Gran's bed with the Christmas presents on the covers, and how her eyes shone when she opened the parcel and saw the doll. Maybe they shone even brighter when Gran opened her present.

And on the big round table, candles were burning in the red candlesticks; and there was the big Christmas dinner that Susy had cooked—though of course Gran had been saying how could she do everything. And Susy sang many Christmas carols for Gran and Gran wagged her head from side to side and said, "Oh my, what a lovely blessed Christmas!"

When finally Susy crept under the covers of her kitchen bench bed that Christmas night, she was so sleepy that she wanted most of all to go to sleep right there and then. She tripped over the words as she said the part about the angel walking outside the house at night. She threw a quick glance out of the window at the garden. It was snowing out there. Everything was so utterly white.

"But, Gran!" exclaimed Susy. "Did you know that the whole garden is full of angels!"

Now, Gran was in the room with windows facing the street but she wagged her head anyway and said,

"Yes, yes, the whole garden is full of angels."

One minute later Susy Spry was asleep.

Astrid Lindgren

Nelson Mandela

A SON OF the chief of the Tembu tribe, politician Nelson Mandela was born in 1918 in South Africa. He was a lawyer in Johannesburg, then joined the African National Congress in 1944. For the next twenty years Mandela directed a campaign of defiance against the South African government and its racist policies. In 1964 he was sentenced to life imprisonment for political offences. As a result of substantial international pressure, Mandela was finally released in 1990, and he was elected president of the ANC the following year. South Africa's leader received the Nobel Peace Prize in 1993.

Letter to
My Grandchild

Even in the lowest forms of animal, basic instincts marshal adults to protect their young. And even before the modern rules of war were established, armed conflict was somehow managed to cause as little destruction as possible to women and children. But today, children and civilians are deliberately targeted in combat and teenagers who are barely able to judge right from wrong are recruited to use weapons.

The irony of our age is that while the scientific achievements of science have propelled humanity to a breadth and depth of civilization hitherto unimagined, we must nevertheless invoke the most basic instincts to attain normalcy and rationality in our behavior.

We might not have witnessed the worst of such privations, but because we seek the happiness and comfort of children and because we seek a better life in a better world, we will join hands with you to ensure that this will come to an end.

Nelson Mandela

Martina Navratilova

TENNIS STAR MARTINA Navratilova was born in Prague in 1956. She defected to the United States in 1975. The winner of a record 9 singles titles at Wimbledon, she won a total of 167 singles titles in her long reign as tennis's top female player.

Navratilova has become known as a spokesperson on several social issues, notably gay rights, animals rights, and ecology. She is also the author of an autobiography, and she has cowritten a novel.

Letter to
My Grandchild

my dear grandchild

what do i wish for you in your lifetime?

    i wish you love, inner peace, happiness, world peace, a healthy planet for starters.

    now—how do you go about getting those?

    love—that is an "easy" one. You give love and sooner or later you will get love back.

    the inner peace you get from giving love, especially unconditional love. It's a nice side effect—see—you get two for the price of one.

    happiness—that needs to come from within—you can get some from others—a lover, friend, family—but you must first be happy with your *SELF*—do not depend on others to supply it.

    world peace—not so easy—do your little piece in your community and hopefully more and more people will do that and before we know it we might actually have it— world peace—what a concept. . . .

    a healthy planet—again, do your bit—be aware of how you can make a difference and speak up—make others aware—environmentalist is not a dirty word.

    i wish for you equality—whatever color, sex, nationality you might be—i wish for you an equal opportunity to do whatever your little (big) heart desires.

    and most of all i wish for you to have the courage to be true to yourself, for that is the only way you will be able to realize your full potential and blossom without limits.

    good luck, my darling, go for it and have fun!!!

love, grandma martina.

Shimon Peres

ISRAELI POLITICIAN SHIMON Peres was born in 1923 in Byelorussia and immigrated to Palestine at the age of eleven. Director-general of the Ministry of Defense at the age of twenty-nine, Peres's achievements include the establishment of Israel's military and aviation industries, as well as its nuclear program. In 1965 he left the ruling Mapai party and became secretary-general of Rafi; three years later he was instrumental in reuniting these Labor factions. A member of the Knesset since 1959, Peres has served two nonconsecutive terms as prime minister of Israel, 1984–86 and 1995–96.

In 1994, Peres won the Nobel Peace Prize with Yitzhak Rabin and Yasser Arafat.

*Letter to
My Grandchild*

From the moment a child is born, he must be taught that life is much too short to be wasted on anger and injustice.

Recently, I received a letter from a crippled young boy who has spent all his life in a wheelchair. He said he wanted to express a personal feeling that he thought might apply to all human beings.

He wrote: "It seems to me that anyone who sees me thinks that what I want most in this world is to be able to get off the wheelchair, yet the truth is that I'm terrified to stand on my feet. The very thought that I will have to face the world and the people in it in an unfamiliar situation frightens me very much."

There is a girl I know, he added, who has been blind from birth and she told me once that she was afraid to think what would happen to her if God suddenly granted her the ability to see. She said that there was nothing she wanted more than to see the light of a new dawn, but admitted to being terrified of experiencing it.

And the boy added that in fact we were all born handicapped in one way or another. That we were all afraid to get off our wheelchair and walk on our own and accept responsibility for ourselves.

I read the boy's letter in our parliament. The boy sat in the gallery, listening, while many were moved to tears. The boy's mother then wrote to me that after the speech the boy rose from his wheelchair for the first time in his life and stood on his feet. For me, that was one of the most moving moments that I had ever experienced. A disabled boy rising up from his wheelchair.

It is so clear that we could all be much healthier than we feel, and less blind than we have been accustomed to. As a grandfather, not just as a father, I would like to grant my

Letter to
My Grandchild

grandchildren both those things, that they could stand on their own feet and see with their own eyes.

To stand on their feet in order to walk the right path, and to see with their eyes lights, not just shadows, in our world.

They may not be applauded by anyone, but they will be able to enrich their surrounding, contribute to their society and offer their successors an improved world. A world that does not glorify bloodshed, and believes that every little child is a whole new world to be discovered; that he deserves all human resources and blessings. That is not history, but this is our future.

Shimon Peres

Aleksandar
Soknić

WRITER ALEKSANDAR SOKNIĆ was born
in Sarajevo in 1953. He received his degree in English language and literature at the
University of Sarajevo and is a member of the Association of Writers of Yugoslavia. He
has published a book of short stories, *Wasting Sense,* and three books of poems: *Labyrinth,
The Race,* and *A Moment Before the Storm. Soknić* is blind and lives as a refugee in Belgrade.

*Letter to
My Grandchild*

My dear grandchild,

I'm now far away from you, in a nice European town, but I'll soon come back home. I'm very impatient to see you again, to go for a walk with you in our park, or to enjoy together looking at some of your beautiful picture books. I'm now drinking a cup of tea, looking through a window at wonderful fields in a valley full of flowers and many smiling fruitful trees, but you are in my thoughts. When I get back, we'll visit the zoo in our town, we'll have a nice time. I'll also make a big fruitcake for you.

My beloved grandson,

Sometimes I wake up in the middle of the night and imagine that you are beside me. I know you are dreaming a big blue star high above with which you are talking and the star gives you all necessary explanations to your numerous questions.

Tomorrow I'm going to buy you a great picture book with many colorful animals and lots of funny spaceships. Also I'm going to bring you some toys that you like.

My dear grandson,

You should be happy in your childhood, you should enjoy every hour and every day of it, and when you grow up, maybe you'll be an actor, a painter, or a writer. Maybe you'll be a bank manager, a scientist, or a teacher. And, in any case, you'll have enough courage to overcome all difficulties that may appear in the future, you'll be enough clever to avoid all life's traps, and enough tender to attract the hearts of other people. When you grow up, you'll travel to many countries, improve your knowledge about the world, and make always friends with good and interesting people.

My dear grandchild, my beloved grandson,

Lord God bless you. In my prayers I always pray for your good health, for your happiness, and for a lightful path in your life.

Letter to
My Grandchild

I believe we'll be soon together and have much time for our joyful talking and playing with the new toys and the picture books.

At the end of this letter, once again I send you all my love and wish you all the best.

Looking forward to spending a lot of nice days with you.

Kissing your smiling cheeks,

always yours,

with greatest love,

Your Grandfather L.

**Karlheinz
Stockhausen**

COMPOSER AND CONDUCTOR

Karlheinz Stockhausen was born in Germany in 1928 and studied at the universities of Köln and Bonn. From an early age he experimented with electronic music, and in 1953 he helped found Cologne's important Electronic Music Studio. One of the most prominent avant-garde composers of the mid-twentieth century, Stockhausen has written over 250 works and released more than 100 records. He has also been a proponent of "intuitive" music, in which musicians are presented with a sketch and improvise from it. His works include *Time Measure* and the multimedia work *Beethausen, opus 1970, von Stockhausen.*

Dear Grandchildren,

Now there are eleven of you: five young Norwegians, three young French children, three young Germans. Greetings from your *Heika-Sirius.*

Yesterday I imagined what I would select for Christmas this year. In my mind's eye I saw for each of you an angel. This morning I was in a small shop in Wipperfürth which sells music staff paper and nativity figures. I have already found five angels playing music instruments, a little boy praying, two little girls praying—all of them very beautifully carved out of wood—and have dedicated them beneath their little feet. I want to look for three more angels, so that I have all eleven and can send them to you. This year namely, I will be conducting the Symphony Orchestra of the Frankfurt Radio every day for all of December until Christmas eve. That is why I have already prepared something for each of you. Naturally you will, as usual, also receive something else which has to do with music.

How are the eleven *clapper-storks*[1] from last Christmas?

---

[1]The German word *Klapperstorch* means, literally, "clapper-stork," the special designation used by parents and children for the storks who bring the babies and clapper with their beaks.

Suja, your mother and aunt will be arriving from Caen this evening with Till, Lelia and Cosima, to spend a week with me. I am very happy and have several surprises waiting. Suja can then describe her trip to India, and the three French grandchildren can tell me about their summer vacation in Norway which you all spent together on the beach. I am very keen to know!

When you receive the angels and other figures, please place them where you always do your homework and practice. It would be wonderful if each day for your whole life you would pray to your guardian angel, as I do several times every day. Recently, I have prayed even more than usual because so many plans for next year went wrong. Last week I even prayed to *MICHAEL* on several days, for good weather because we are building a little *House of Light* in the forest, and if it had rained everything would have been spoiled. But the sun came out, even though many had said it would rain: *MICHAEL* heard me!

Also the worst impossibilities—the world premiere of my new work for choir, *World-Parliament*, which was to have been on October 26th in Stuttgart after many rehearsals, and the premiere of the opera *Friday from Light* from March 27th to 30th next year at the Leipzig Opera—have finally become possible again through angelic assistance: *World-Parliament* will now be world premiered next year on February 3rd, and *Friday from Light* on September 12th. How the musicians, the children of the Leipzig children's choir and the children's orchestra have trembled with me!

Now we must have more patience and rehearse much longer, but I believe that it will be even better than originally planned.

I hope that all of you will come to Leipzig again—as you did for *Tuesday from Light.* There are many surprises—magic sounds—dirty tricks (oh boy!)—spooky events— eerie things—a lot of funny happenings—very beautiful moments!

A musikiss for each of you
sent by your Heika-Sirius

Desmond M. Tutu

ARCHBISHOP AND PROMOTER of civil rights Desmond M. Tutu was born in 1931 in South Africa. In 1978 he became the first black general secretary of the South African Council of Churches. He has been a lecturer at colleges and universities around the world, receiving numerous honors and awards. Bishop Tutu received the Nobel Peace Prize in 1984.

Dear ones,

I am a part of you and you will always be a part of me. I think I have the better deal!

Through your parents you too are my children and I love you more than you can ever imagine. The two most precious gifts are life and love. God gives us life and what he wants most of all is for us to be happy. The secret of finding happiness is to make others happy. It is not always easy to love everyone but you don't have to love someone or even like someone to care about them. To care whether they are hungry or sad. It is that caring love that God wants us to have for each other and for the world.

The world is the most beautiful place. Enjoy it, and fill it with laughter and love and you will make God smile.

God bless you,
Desmond M. Tutu

**Liv
Ullmann**

THE NORWEGIAN ACTRESS Liv Ullmann was born in 1938. Making her stage debut in 1957, Ullmann became internationally known through her work with Swedish film director Ingmar Bergman on the film and television series *Scenes from a Marriage*. Liv Ullmann directed her first film, *Sofie,* in 1992, and last year she directed Ingmar Bergman's *Intimate Conversations*. Throughout her career, Liv Ullmann has been active in humanitarian work, and in 1980 she was appointed goodwill ambassador of UNICEF.

What do I wish for you, my dear little grandson—only three months old?

I wish Hope for you.

That you will give people hope.

I wish Compassion for you.

That you will show people compassion.

What kind of Women do I want for you? I wish for you women who take pride in womanhood because it includes the talent for embracing.

I wish for you women who will dare to emphasize their uniqueness—cherish it— and who will learn never to undervalue themselves. And I wish for you the ability to recognize them, and salute their ability to be soft enough to lean on.

What kind of Men do I wish for you? I wish for you men who dismiss the idea that strength is measured by their ability to conquer and dominate.

I wish for you men who aim to reinterpret the world and question dominant stereotypes, men who understand that visions are more important than slogans. And I wish for you the ability to share with them an enlightened spirit—descriptive of real feelings—which will linger with, and be a part of them, forever.

What kind of World do I wish for you? I wish for you a world where man and woman never make an important decision without including the consequences of this decision on the Seventh Generation to come.

I trust in your power as a grown man—to trace the time when you were of a pure heart—when you painted strange images and spoke with flowers. When you believed you were part of the Whole. When you touched without fear.

There are opportunities waiting for you, my grandson.

Voices out there you must listen to.

Letter to
My Grandchild

Human beings out there in the world who will never vote for you or applaud you or honor you.

Who will simply need you.

You will finally be described by how you reacted to these needs.

The finished portrait of yourself—the one you can never change, however beautifully ornamented the frame—will encompass the care and the vision you enacted on behalf of others. And how you, through their destinies, learned to recognize yourself.

Finally, I hope that you will know that you are never a witness only. You are a participant, and as such your times will be counted in heartbeats, not in possessions.

My sweet grandson—of three short months: May you in life give room to your feelings—risk being hurt—and learn about love.

Liv Ullmann

**Jørn
Utzon**

ARCHITECT JØRN UTZON was born in 1918 in Denmark. He was initially inspired by Alvar Alto and studied in Helsinki, Finland. Best known for his design of the Sydney Opera House in 1957, his other major projects include the National Assembly building in Kuwait, the Zurich Schauspielhaus, and the Basvaard church in Copenhagen. Jørn Utzon is also known for his designs of domestic houses and has received several international prizes. The text for this book is fictitious, and was written by Jeppe Utzon, the grandson of Jørn Utzon.

*Letter to
My Grandchild*

Dear Grandson:

Right now, which it is not, I am sitting in my own space in the attic of my father's house. The attic is the place where you put things that does not smell. My grandfather did that when this house was his. It is more likely that he made my father do it, though. No matter. What matters is that he was very good at it. He was a natural. As a result there is incredible amounts of my grandfather's things stored up here. Also he was a very smart man because he sold the house furnished. Buying a house furnished usually means that you get all the things that would otherwise have been thrown out. But you get them cheap. I wish my father could have been smarter. Or maybe he was just being nice, because, when I think about it, he fooled me into doing the attic which is by far the worst part. Son, if you would like to have your own room . . . a whole floor to yourself . . . and so on. This brings me back to now. I have been at it for half a day and all I have managed to do so far is clear an area which could not even hold a bed. This is the pessimistic interpretation though. An optimist would say that in an attic containing fifty years' accumulated collectibles I have undone seven years in just half a day.

Whether you see it one way or the other is not important (or maybe it is exactly what is). The fact of the matter is that I have become a part of it. In a week's time most of my grandfather's things will be in a different location altogether. Then I will start my own little accumulation. Maybe, hopefully, it will not be the same things and not the same attic, but I am sure that somehow and someday you are going to have to sort through things which are mine. Not quite as many, though. So I am part of the vicious circle and now I made you part of it too. Which brings me to why I wrote this letter. While I have been creating space I have been thinking about matter—my grandfather. Who and how he was and why did he collect these things. What I have found out I already knew. I know him only as an old man labelled grandfather. Not what he was like when he was young. How he felt and what he thought. I never knew him as a friend. Then I got afraid that my grandchildren will know as little about me as I know about my grandfather. Will they forget that I was young too. I wanted you to know me before I am labelled grandfather or even father and this is now. So instead of telling you the secret location of the time machine, I will cross time in this letter. It is the introduction to a diary of a kind in which I will write infrequently so that you may know me when I am young. I have delayed it slightly, however, because that is part of the plan.

Jeppe Utzon

Letter to
My Grandchild

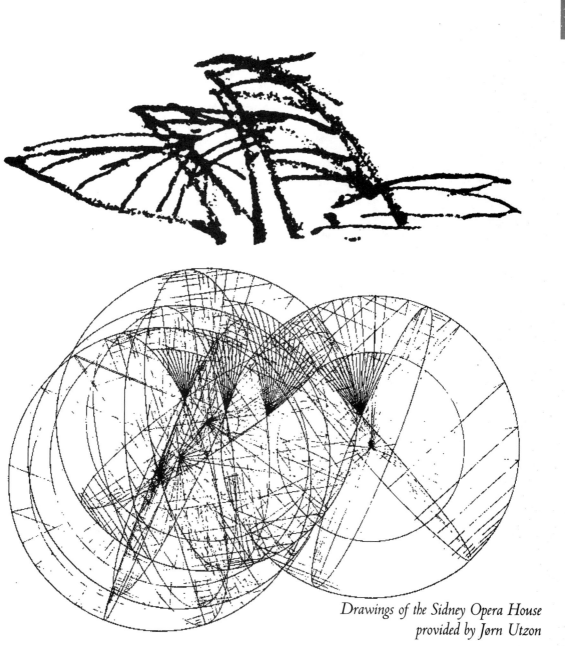

*Drawings of the Sidney Opera House
provided by Jørn Utzon*

**Lech
Wałęsa**

POLISH LABOR UNION activist and president of Poland between 1990 and 1995, Lech Wałęsa was a founding member and chairman of the independent trade union Solidarity. Arrested during several strikes in the early 1980s, he led Solidarity's negotiations with Poland's Communist government in 1988 and 1989. He received the Nobel Peace Prize in 1983, and his autobiography, *A Way of Hope,* was published in 1987.

My dear grandson,

I want you to respect me and not to follow in my footsteps.

I want you to understand what it fell to me to do; I want you to know that my dedication, my actions, and my sacrifices were not in vain. I want you to believe that what it fell to me to do was worth the doing, and that my efforts were to some avail. I hope that you will come to understand the motives that lay behind what I did and that you will come to share them. I want you to understand me, value me, and even—forgive me, dear grandson—envy me a little.

Yet I don't want you to follow in my footsteps. I don't want you to have to do what I had to do. I came into the world during the most terrible of wars; you were born in peacetime. It's my wish that that difference should always remain. That the things for which I had to fight, for which I was sent to prison, and for which I was persecuted should be for you an inalienable right. That you should live in a better, more perfect world.

But remember that what is worth dying for is also worth living for; that life should have its purpose; and that one day you'll have a grandson to whom you'll have to be able to say that you lived an upright life.

May God and my blessing go with you.

L. W.

Andrew Weil

DOCTOR AND WRITER Andrew Weil, a graduate of Harvard College and Harvard Medical School, has worked for the National Institute of Mental Health and was a research associate in ethnopharmacology at Harvard Botanical Museum. As a fellow of the Institute of Current World Affairs, he has traveled extensively throughout the world collecting information about medical plants and healing. He is the founder of the Center for Integrative Medicine in Tucson, Arizona, and director of the Program in Integrative Medicine at the University of Arizona. Dr. Weil's most recent book—his seventh—is *Eight Weeks to Optimum Health.*

Letter to
My Grandchild

To My Grandchildren:

Health is your most precious possession, but you will not appreciate it until you lose it. Your bodies have a remarkable natural ability to maintain and heal themselves. It is up to you to protect that ability. The choices you make about how to live—for example how you eat, how you exercise, how you handle stress, how you use your minds—all will influence your health and healing and determine the shape you will be in later in life.

Young bodies are very resilient and forgiving—so much so that it is hard for you to see that unhealthy habits have consequences. Many people first experience serious breakdowns in health in middle age and think they come out of the blue. In fact, the breakdowns are often the results of years of unhealthy living, appearing when youthful resilience begins to go. As a doctor I have seen so many grown-ups suffer from diseases that could have been avoided if people, early enough in life, had made better choices about how to live in order to protect their natural healing ability.

I urge you to seek out good information on diet, exercise, and the rest, and then to act on it. You will meet people who think that healthy living and fun living are opposites. Don't believe them! It is perfectly possible to get as much fun and pleasure from a healthy lifestyle as an unhealthy one—maybe more. And remember: the easiest way to develop the habits you want is to spend more time with people who have them.

Not only do I not want you to suffer from preventable diseases, I also want you to enjoy optimum health and be good role models for your children. The more you dedicate yourself to these goals, the happier and healthier your world will be.

With all my love,
Andrew Weil, MD

**Fay
Weldon**

FAY WELDON WAS born in England in 1933 and raised in New Zealand. She is the author of twenty-one novels, including *Worst Fears, Splitting,* and *The Life and Loves of a She-Devil.* She lives in London.

*Letter to
My Grandchild*

A fax came up on my machine the other day; inch by slow inch it revealed itself as an ultrasonic scan of you in the womb, six months on from conception, transmitted via your father's, my son's, computer. It went to all friends and family members sufficiently *au fait* with technological matters to receive it. "Hi there!" you said, in effect, three months before your birth, "Hi there, here I am, in this brand-new world you have created for me. No sooner here, than recorded. Those that can see, let them see."

This picture of your unborn self came as both blessing and shock: the sheer marvel of new life was sufficient to overcome its translation into the digital world and out again, and leave a smile of pleasure behind. The shock was the realisation of how little mystery we have left in ourselves, yet how much mystery remains. There you were, all spirit, in grainy black and white: your temperament and disposition already clear in the foetal curl, the thumb in the mouth, a matter of body language; I read you as determined, cheerful, and very much in charge of the processes that formed you. You are no one's bit part player, you play no minor role in someone else's drama; you are the drama itself, and you know it.

I already know you are a girl, that your name will be Ella. I know your antecedents. You take half your genetic material from your father, who has half of mine and half his father's: half from your mother's side, likewise, and back in exponential halvings to Mother Eve out of Africa some half a million years back. (If we are to believe Richard Dawkins, geneticist and evolutionary theoretician, that is, who writes so brilliantly about the stream of developing life through the aeons, and not some creationist, who'd have us all in God's image and sprung ready made from Adam's rib. But all notions, all tales of creation mythology, tell of equal marvels: don't you worry about the origin of life for the time being. Enough just to *be*, and glow at us from the womb.) On your father's side you come from English stock out of the Viking invasion, a thousand years ago, and Jewish immigration out of Eastern Europe at the turn of the century: on your mother's side you are part English, part Italian. We are all world citizens, remember that: the liveliest people are the least likely to stay where they were born. So see no virtue in staying home: choose for your children a father most likely to startle your parents. This way you serve nature's plan for diversity, though it may not make for a tranquil existence. And what is tranquillity but boredom.

Wherever you look in your family history you will find the demimonde: musicians, painters, sculptors, writers, poets, filmmakers, people often disgraced, sometimes notable. Add to those a handful of entrepreneurs, politicians. There is without a doubt a restless tendency in the family, especially in the women. My grandmother, born in 1878, would tell me of her grandmother, Mary Frances, born in 1841, a sculptress, who left her husband to earn her own living writing poems about the villainy of men.

Between us we have made a world for you in which it is more difficult for men to be villainous than it used to be. As a corollary, alas, you will be expected to earn your own living. I hope for your sake you will find an easy way of doing it: that you will have some special skill which will be recognised and well rewarded, so you have energy left over for love. I hope you are pretty because good-looking women have an easier time and can pick and choose in life; but not too pretty, so you don't bother to develop empathy with others. To this end my mother's generation never praised little girls for their looks, and made expressions of love dependent upon good behaviour: your mother's generation find it natural to say to their daughters, "How pretty you look" and to demonstrate love even when, especially when, it is least deserved. Today's child is superbly confident; and I'm sure I wish it for you, even though wondering where it will lead. My generation spent its childhood waiting and preparing for adulthood: yours spends its living now with the adult world in servitude. Lucky old you.

I do not want you to be a feminist, if by feminist is meant a woman who derides and despises men, in the same way as it was once customary for men to deride and despise women. I want you to be a feminist in the sense that you see yourself as a person first and of a certain gender second: I want you to live in a world in which this is

Letter to
My Grandchild

possible. I want you to have children and make me a great-grandmother, no matter how much I know rationally that these days, in the professional classes, it's sheer folly for a girl to have babies. All expense, making-do, child care, and anxiety. I am glad your mother had sense enough to disregard all sensible advice, so now you lie sucking your thumb and feeding up on faxes all over the land, declaring your unborn presence amongst us.

Already, Ella, I feel you are capable of having orchestrated the whole technological world into existence, the better to make the ingenious and unforgettable entrance by fax into it. You take after your charismatic father in this. He was always one for an entrance.

I want you to have your cake and eat it too. I want you to like men but be able to be faithful and ask me to the wedding: I've never been to a white wedding, certainly not my own. Let me stagger on my decrepit legs to yours. My mother, your great-grandmother, sees our function in the world as that of scavengers. God flew off leaving the debris of creation behind, and the task of the human race is to sort through the mess, salvaging what is good, waste-not-want-notting. We are, she declares, the salvage team of the universe. I hope you will leave the world a better place than when you entered it, but not to be too earnest about it. I hope you will be able to make others laugh; and that rooms light up when you come into them. I want you to be head-girl of your school, and get a first in Economics and be Miss World as well, if you choose to. I want you to solve every paradox that ever puzzled me.

Over to you, Ella. I'm quite sure, from the way you suck your thumb, contemplate existence, and conserve your energy for the great push into the bright, dangerous life of the world, that you'll live up to our expectations and be known through history as the solver of GUM, the Great Universal Mystery, and GUP, the Great Universal Paradox: why we are born in the first place, and why it's so difficult once we're here. May you be both High Priestess and Chief Scientist. Unto us a child is born. Welcome.

Fay Weldon

Elie Wiesel

WRITER AND PROFESSOR Elie Wiesel was born in 1928 in Romania to Jewish parents. After World War II, he lived in Paris for a while, then settled in the United States. His boyhood experiences in a Nazi concentration camp are vividly described in his book *Night*.

Wiesel won the Nobel Peace Prize in 1986. He is a professor at Boston University.

Letter to My Grandchild

To Liv's grandchild:

I knew your grandmother before you. I was younger at the time, but she is always young. And yet there is something in her that makes her stronger than her years. Something compelling. And touching.

I won't speak to you of her talent, which is great, if not unique. I want to speak to you of her still rarer qualities, those which brought her close to children your age who are less fortunate than you, to those who suffer from hunger, from fear, from sickness, or, simply, from loneliness.

I saw her in a camp for Cambodian refugees. Constantly surrounded by children whose eyes were full of sad memories, she knew how to comfort them with a touch, with a word, with a smile. She found their grief unbearable. She would not leave them thirsting for hope. And then, I would see them transformed by her presence.

It was because she loved children, your grandmother. She loved them with fervor and tenderness, as she alone knew how to love. If the unfortunate children of this unbalanced, crazy, and dark world could elect a queen, they would certainly place the crown on her head. Because they loved her with all the passion of their youth.

And we love her as well.

Elie Wiesel

Simon
Wiesenthal

SIMON WIESENTHAL WAS born in Austria in 1908 and graduated as an architect. During World War II, he was sent to a concentration camp by the Nazis. After the war, he founded the Jewish Documentation Center in Vienna, and he has been a leading figure in the attempts to track down and prosecute former Nazi war criminals.

*Letter to
My Grandchild*

My dear grandchildren!

In four years our century comes to an end. Since I was born in 1908, I have experienced everything there was to experience in this century. Looking back, I call it the "Criminal Century": there were two World Wars; when just a child, I was a refugee, and as an adult, I was again a refugee. Most of our family did not die by natural means, but rather had to suffer a violent death at the hands of criminals.

When I think about the coming century—which I will hardly experience—and reflect upon how it ought to differ from the one which is coming to an end, I continually hope that you may be spared what we, your grandparents, had to experience. Your mother bears the same first name as that of your two great-grandmothers, so that they—as is the custom for us Jews—may live on in their descendants.

Your grandmother and I are survivors, and as such are not only obligated to the dead, but also to the coming generations. We must pass on our experiences to you so that you can learn from them, for I am of the conviction: "Information is Defense."

It is not enough that everything has already been recorded in books, because one cannot question a book as one can a human being. A witness must be a "living" witness. For this reason, I have admonished, again and again, in assemblies of survivors at which I have spoken; "You have children. You have grandchildren. Your neighbors have children—you must speak to them. You must tell them everything you have experienced, and your retelling will provoke them to tell others. Only in oral telling does the memory remain living."

As you know, after my liberation, I have continually sought speech with young people, and through my lectures at universities in many countries of the world I have spoken to thousands. I would stand before well-dressed, well-nourished, happy young people and suddenly I would ask myself: how could I make someone who has never suffered hunger or cold in his life understand how much, in those days, a slice of bread, a piece of cabbage, or a jacket meant? How can I convey to one who only knows death from reading the newspaper what one feels who sees and knows the smoke over a crematorium: the oily, sweet smell that comes from humans who just yesterday marched in a long column through the camp streets? With what words could I describe to these young people the pain of a mother whose child is torn from her arms and thrown with those who are certain for the gas chamber?

I fear that it is impossible to impart all these experiences. We can speak and form our memories into words. But these words, even when our listeners eagerly take them in, do not become reality in their minds. What happened in the Third Reich defies the power of comprehension.

We, your grandparents, in the face of all objections, have the responsibility to express to you and our young listeners how singular, how incomprehensible, and how extraordinary the time of the Holocaust was. However, by doing so, we make it more difficult for you to accept our depictions as truth and reality. The incomprehensible remains incomprehensible.

My dear grandchildren, I must confess that we, your grandparents, also committed a series of mistakes. Among these mistakes, we believed that we could fight against hatred of the Jews alone, and that we would earn attention through our achievements. Also count among the mistakes that, after 2,000 years, we still had not comprehended that we are always the first victims of discord—wherever a majority is incited against a minority, in the end the Jew is hammered to the cross. And add to these mistakes that we watched and we waited, as long as we could still get by.

We also could not believe that the people of Schiller and Goethe could submit themselves to a Hitler or Himmler. Moreover, the Jews in Eastern Europe were extremely Germanophilic because they were the bearers of German culture in this region. When they were expelled from Germany centuries before, they had taken their language, namely, middle-high German, with them and preserved it. (The Spanish Jews did the same thing, by the way, when they took with them the old Castilian, as Ladino, after they were expelled from Spain.)

Letter to
My Grandchild

Of course, I still remember that the majority of books in the bookcase in our apartment in Buczacz were German. When my mother, your great-grandmother, wanted to communicate something really important to me, she would take a German classic in her hand and say to me: "Look, this can much better express what I want to say to you."

And we also erred in believing that one who had read Goethe would not read that Nazi smear-sheet, the *Stürmer*.

It is sometimes asserted that there is no chance the National Socialism of Hitler's kind will return. There could perhaps be other sorts of fascism, which would perhaps lead to other persecutions, but never again like those of the Third Reich. I, too, hope this is so, but I have learned that control is better than trust.

When hate and sadism gird themselves with modern technology, the inferno may break out anew anywhere. This combination of hate and technology is the greatest danger that man exposes himself to. It encompasses not only the great technology of the atom bomb, but also the little technologies of daily life: I know people who sit for hours before the television screen because they have failed to learn how to communicate with one another. Soon, we will no longer have to learn foreign languages because there will be pocket computers which we can speak into in our own language and which will translate our words into foreign speech. More and more, human beings will make themselves understood to one another by means of a computer. Sometimes I have a fearful vision that one day computers will be able to speak to one another without human beings at all.

My dear grandchildren, we have led many a long and good conversation with one another since you were old enough to start gradually learning of my experiences under Nazi domination. I hope that you will take this dialogue with you into the new century, and that through the knowledge of the perils which I have passed on to you, you will be better protected from them.

With love,
Your grandfather